KIDS'
Paper
Air
Plane
BOOK

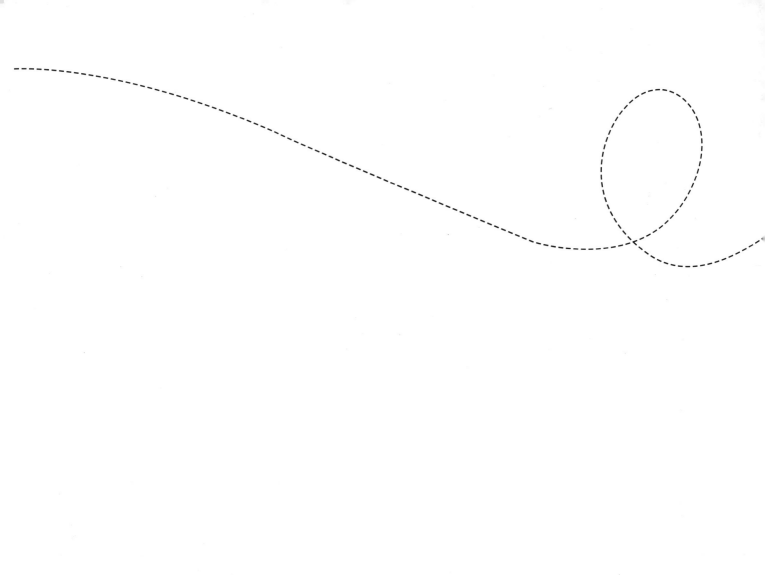

KIDS'
Paper
Air
Plane
BOOK

WRITTEN BY KEN BLACKBURN
PLANES ENGINEERED BY
KEN BLACKBURN & JEFF LAMMERS

KÖNEMANN

THIS BOOK WAS MADE POSSIBLE BY THE DIRECT AND INDIRECT HELP OF MANY PEOPLE. IN PARTICULAR WE WOULD LIKE TO THANK:

Our parents, Paul and Lynn Blackburn and Jerry and Angie Lammers, and Aunt Dolores, for a lifetime of guidance, help, and support.

Our wives, Sarah Blackburn and Karen Lammers, for their help and for their encouragement in urging us to follow our dreams.

Jackie (Blackburn) Tyson for her encouragement and help in starting Ken's writing career.

John David for his help rendering the folding instructions.

All our teachers whose guidance in such diverse subjects as science, English, and biomechanics provided the foundation that enabled us to write this book.

Ken's college friends for their kick in the pants and help in setting the world record.

All the people at Workman Publishing who worked hard to make this book a reality. In particular we want to thank Peter Workman for believing in us, our editor Margot Herrera for transforming a rough stone into a polished diamond, the designers Lisa Hollander and Lori S. Malkin, and all the illustrators whose work brings the book alive.

Cover design: Lisa Hollander
Interior design: Lisa Hollander and Lori S. Malkin
Black and white illustrations: Bob Byrd
Cover and interior photographs: Walt Chrynwski
Plane graphics: Saturn Rocket, Flying Saucer, Aerobat, Count, Dragon Ring, Blue Angels and Thunderbirds, Slice, F-15 by Shi Chen; Pirate's Secret, Robo-Chopper, Great White and Airport Poster by Mark Monlux; World Record Paper Airplane by Janice McDonnell; S.S. Explorer and Thunderbolt by Maurice Kessler; Butterfly by Burton Morris; Glider by Greg Lewis.

First published by
Workman Publishing Company, Inc.
708 Broadway
New York, NY 10003-9555

Copyright © of this edition
Könemann Verlagsgesellschaft mbH
Bonner Strasse 126, D-50968 Cologne

Production: Ursula Schümer
Printing and Binding: Kossuth Printing House Co., Budapest

Printed in Hungary

ISBN 3-8290-2767-2

10 9 8 7 6 5 4 3 2

Flip the pages at the top corner of this book to see where this plane goes next.

Contents

WHY PAPER AIRPLANES FLY . . .
AND WHY THEY CRASH 6

HOW I SET THE GUINNESS
WORLD RECORD 9

FOLDING AND FLYING
YOUR PLANES 11

A FIELD GUIDE TO
COMMON AIRCRAFT 16

GREAT GAMES
TO PLAY INDOORS 18

FEARLESS OUTDOOR FLYING 21

HOW TO BE A STUNT PILOT 23

SETTING UP A PAPER
AIRPLANE CONTEST 26

PAPER AIRPLANE
PILOT'S LICENSE 29

HOW TO FOLD, FIX,
AND FLY THE PLANES
IN THIS BOOK 31
The Count 32
Pirate's Secret 34
The Slice 36
The Glider 38
Robo-Chopper 40
Aerobat 42
The S.S. Explorer 44
The Butterfly 46
The Thunderbolt 48
Dragon Ring 50
Blue Angels and
Thunderbirds 52
Saturn Rocket 54
The World Record
Paper Airplane 56
Flying Saucer 58
The Great White 60
The F-15 62

THE FLIGHT LOG 64

THE PLANES THEMSELVES 65

Why Paper Airplanes Fly...and Why They Crash

Did you ever wonder how a bird or an airplane stays in the air? Studying two sheets of paper can help you understand. A wadded-up piece of paper drops to the ground when thrown, while another piece folded into a paper airplane floats gracefully across the room. The reason for this has to do with the forces of gravity and lift.

GRAVITY AND LIFT

Each piece of paper weighs the same, so **gravity** pulls downward the same amount on each. The difference is the paper airplane has wings that create **lift**, which keeps the plane in the air as if it had an invisible hand holding it up. The wadded-up paper has nothing to hold it in the air, so it quickly drops to the floor.

The wings of all birds and airplanes work the

THE FOUR FORCES OF AERODYNAMICS

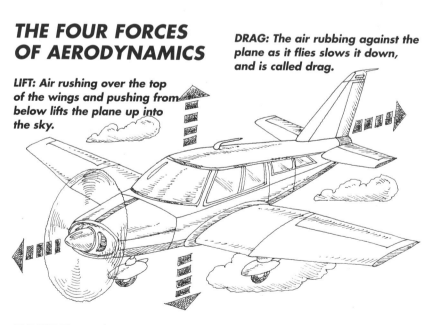

LIFT: Air rushing over the top of the wings and pushing from below lifts the plane up into the sky.

DRAG: The air rubbing against the plane as it flies slows it down, and is called drag.

THRUST: The engine pushes the plane forward through the air. This force is called thrust.

GRAVITY: Gravity pulls the plane down toward Earth.

LIFT IN ACTION

Aerodynamics are hard to understand, even if you're a pilot or have studied the subject for years. To help make it clearer, here's an activity that will show lift in action.

Take a regular sheet of paper and find a room big enough for you to spin around and around. Stand in an open space and hold your arms straight out with one hand on top of the paper and the other on the bottom. Your thumbs should be pointed in the direction you want to spin. For example, if you want to spin toward the right, your left hand should be on top and your right hand on the bottom. Point your thumbs slightly toward the ceiling.

Start spinning. After you've gotten going, remove the hand that's under the paper. The paper will not fall to the ground! The lift from the air rushing over the paper keeps it in place. If you stop spinning, the paper will fall to the floor. The faster you spin, the more lift you create.

To see how an angle affects lift, after you have removed your hand from under the paper, slowly point the thumb of your other hand about halfway up toward the ceiling. When you lower your thumb, you can feel the lift decrease. If you lower it far enough, eventually the paper will drop to the floor.

---

same way. As a wing moves through the air, its front edge is angled up a little bit. Air passing under the wing is slowed down when it rams into the bottom of the wing, creating pressure, which pushes the wing up. At the same time, the air flowing over the top of the wing speeds up, lessening pressure and creating a suction that pulls up on the wing. Together, the two forces are called lift. The more the wing is angled up, the more lift it creates, until it reaches the stall angle. A stall is when the wing is at too high an angle for the air to flow smoothly over the top. When the wing stalls, it can no longer create much lift and the airplane will crash.

DRAG AND THRUST

When anything flies through the air, from a paper airplane to a jet airliner, the air rushing across it rubs against it and tries to slow it down. This is called **drag**. Airplane engines create **thrust**, the push forward that keeps the airplane from slowing down. When an airplane is flying level and thrust is greater than drag, the airplane speeds up. If there is less thrust than drag, the airplane slows down.

As you know, paper airplanes do not have engines. Your throw initially produces the necessary thrust to get your plane moving. Then what keeps it from slowing down? Think of a paper airplane as a coasting bicycle. If you are on level ground and stop peddling (stop producing thrust), the bicycle will slow down (because of drag) and even-

WHAT A DRAG

Drag is a force that slows things down. Try this next activity so you can actually feel drag. Take a regular sheet of paper and find a room that has an open space big enough for you to spin around and around. Stand in the center and hold your arms straight out, clasping the piece of paper vertically between your two hands. Your thumbs should be pointed straight up toward the ceiling.

Start spinning. After you've gotten going, remove the hand in front from the paper. The force pushing the paper against your other hand is drag. As you spin faster, the drag increases and the paper is pushed harder against your hand. Your spinning provides the thrust to keep the paper moving. When you stop spinning (stop providing thrust), the drag quickly brings the paper to a stop, and it drops to the ground.

tually stop. If you coast your bicycle down a hill, gravity becomes the thrust that keeps your bicycle from slowing down. Paper airplanes work like this, too. If you throw your plane straight out, it will slow down. If you throw it very slightly downward, gravity will keep pulling your plane forward as it coasts down an invisible hill.

FAST FACT

Blimps and balloons float in the air for the same reason that corks float in water. The helium in a balloon weighs less than air, just like cork weighs less than water.

WHY PAPER PLANES CRASH

Most paper airplanes that crash actually are able to create enough lift to fly. So why don't they fly? They're unstable. **Stability** keeps planes flying smoothly forward. There are three main types of stability: pitch stability, directional stability, and roll stability.

To have a plane with stable **pitch**, you need weight toward the front. This keeps the plane's nose from pointing too far up or down. **Directional** stability is what keeps the plane flying straight. Like pitch stability, directional stability is improved by keeping the weight of the plane forward. Having a tail or fins at the back of the plane also helps keep it directionally stable.

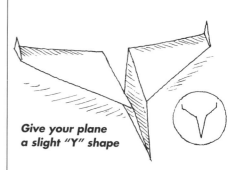

Give your plane a slight "Y" shape

Roll stability keeps the plane's wings level. A plane without roll stability will begin to circle, turning tighter and tighter until it spins down in a vertical dive. To give your plane roll stability, make sure that the wings form a slight "Y" shape with the body.

How I Set the Guinness World Record

Most people don't think they can set a world record. I know. I used to think that way, too. I started making paper airplanes just for the fun of it when I was about seven years old. Over the years, I improved my planes and eventually landed in the *Guinness Book of World Records.*

I have always loved airplanes, and as a kid I made lots of model airplanes. I enjoyed flying them, but didn't like the expense, the building time, and the eventual tree landing or crash. While browsing in the library one day, I discovered several books that showed me how to make some great paper airplanes. I found the best-flying planes were the square-looking ones. I also learned that the real secret to making paper airplanes fly well is the small adjustments you make once you've flown the planes a few times.

Soon I was flying lots of paper airplanes. They flew well, were quick to make, and were just about free. I improved my planes by studying anything I could find about real airplanes, then making changes to my paper models. I even started coming up with my own plane designs.

When I was 13 years old, I designed a new plane that flew really well. I could throw it very high outdoors and watch the wind carry it as it slowly glided to the ground. It soon became my

> ## FAST FACT
> ---
> **T**he longest recorded distance flown by a paper airplane thrown from the ground indoors is 193 feet (more than twice the length of a basketball court). It was thrown by Tony Feltch in La Crosse, Wisconsin, on May 21, 1985.

favorite plane, and I worked constantly to improve it.

When I was 15 years old, my parents gave me a *Guinness Book of World Records* as a gift. I quickly

GUINNESS GUIDELINES

Here are the rules for setting a Guinness World Record for paper airplane time aloft:

1. The flight must take place indoors.

2. The plane must be made from a single sheet of paper that is no larger than 9.84 by 13.90 inches (250 x 353 mm) and weighs no more than 5 ounces (150 grams). Typing or copier paper works great.

3. It's OK to use some tape or glue.

4. The plane must be thrown from level ground. The stopwatch must start when you release the plane, and end when the plane touches anything (the floor, a wall, a chair . . .).

5. You're allowed six attempts.

6. You must submit the following to file a record claim:
   • Signed statements from two witnesses saying that they saw you set the record.
   • A newspaper clipping about the event.
   • Color photographs and a continuous video tape of the flight (you must have both).

NOTE: It is not required that a Guinness representative be present.

turned to the section with aircraft records. Among the records was one for paper airplanes. It stated that the longest time a paper airplane had flown over a level surface was 15.0 seconds. I soon realized my paper airplanes would fly nearly that long, so I set a goal to try to break the world record.

After a year of practice and fine-tuning, I gathered my friends, teachers, and a newspaper reporter for a record attempt. My plane flew for almost 25 seconds! I was elated until Guinness informed me the record had to be set indoors. Setting the record had to wait. I needed to find a large enough building to do it in,

and I also needed to practice and improve my throw.

At 20, I was studying to become an aerospace engineer at North Carolina State University. I told some friends about my "almost" record, and they decided they would help me try again. They timed my flights and arranged for a reporter to cover the event.

After a month of practice, we gathered at my college's basketball arena for the attempt. With a camera and a stopwatch ready, I threw my best plane as hard as I could into the upper reaches of the building, only to watch it glide into a cluster of speakers. My best plane, gone forever!

One of my friends found a sheet of copier paper, and I quickly folded another plane. My third throw with this new plane was the best at 16.89 seconds—a new record! After a couple of nervous weeks, the letter I wanted arrived— Guinness approved the record! After five years, I had finally reached my goal.

Since then I have been able to reset my record twice—first at 17.2 seconds, then at 18.8 seconds, where the record stands today. I have had flights of up to 21 seconds in practice sessions, so maybe I'll try again. I'd like to break the 20-second barrier.

Folding and Flying Your Planes

lmost anyone can make paper airplanes, but it helps to know a little about how best to fold them and how to make them fly the way you want. The following guidelines will help you have great flights from the get-go. Tip: If you're a first-time paper airplane pilot, start with either the Slice or the Pirate's Secret. They're excellent fliers, easy to fold, and simple to adjust.

MAKING THE PLANES

The planes in this book are marked with three kinds of lines: solid white lines, dashed lines, and dotted lines. The solid white lines show you where to cut the plane. They're also marked with little pictures of scissors. The dashed lines are what we call "fold-in" lines. This means that these lines will be on the inside of a crease; you will not be able to see them once you make the fold. They are your main folding guides and are numbered in the order you should make the folds. The dotted lines are "fold-away" lines. You'll be able to see them on the outside of the crease when

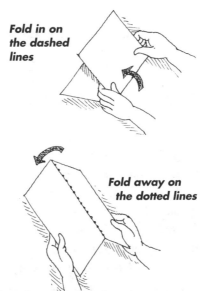

Fold in on the dashed lines

Fold away on the dotted lines

you make your folds. These lines are guides to help you know that you're folding in the right place.

Try to make your creases as sharp as possible. It's smart to run a fingernail over the edge after you make a fold. This will help especially with the planes that have a lot of folds in one area, like the World Record Paper Airplane and the Pirate's Secret.

Don't worry if sometimes your folds are a little off from the dashed and dotted lines. Try your best to fold along the lines, but if they don't match exactly, it's OK. The plane will probably come out fine. Do make sure, however, that your plane's wings are even. If they are different shapes or sizes, it'll be hard to get the plane to fly well.

ADJUSTING THE PLANES

Even if you folded your plane perfectly, there's a good chance that it won't fly well. Why not? Because almost all paper airplanes need a little fine-tuning to fly properly.

FAST AND SLOW Adjusting the elevators is probably the most impor-

tant thing you can do to prevent your plane from diving (when it suddenly swoops to the ground and crashes) or stalling (when it climbs, slows, then dives). Elevator adjustments also let you make the plane fly fast or slowly. The elevators on a paper airplane are usually located at the back edges of the wings. Elevators on real planes are normally

Up elevator

on the back edge of the tail and work the same way as elevators on paper airplanes.

If you find that your

plane is diving and crashing, add up elevator by bending the back edges of the wings up a little.

If you find your plane is stalling, you may have added too much up elevator. Flatten the back edges of the wings.

The more you bend the elevator up, the slower the plane will fly. With proper adjustments you can make it float through the air. Reduce the amount of up elevator for fast flights. Every airplane is different, so it will probably take a few adjustments and throws to fine-tune your plane to fly at the speed you want.

LEFT AND RIGHT Most paper airplanes have a

ELEVATOR EXPERIMENT

Make a paper airplane (the Count or the Pirate's Secret would be good) and throw it without adjusting the elevators. See how it flies. Now bend the elevators up a little and throw it again. Adjust the plane until you get a smooth flight. Keep bending

the elevators up and notice how this makes the plane fly more slowly. Eventually, the elevators will be bent up so much that the plane will stall because it is trying to fly too slowly. The amount of up elevator that makes this happen is different for every plane.

tendency to turn to the right or left when they are first thrown. This can be fixed by adjusting the rudder of the plane. On most paper airplanes, the rudder is the back edge of the body (or fuselage). To adjust it, use your fingers to bend it right or left. Usually you only need to bend it a little, but sometimes you will need to bend it so much that it points directly out to the side.

If your plane isn't flying straight, throw it a few times and watch which way it turns. Then, holding your plane from behind, bend the rudder in the direction you want it to go. For example, if your plane is veering off to the right, bend the rudder a little to the left. If your plane is heading to the left, bend the rudder a little to the right.

If your plane flies straight and you want it to fly to the right, bend the rudder to the right. Likewise, if you want your plane to

Adjusting the rudder

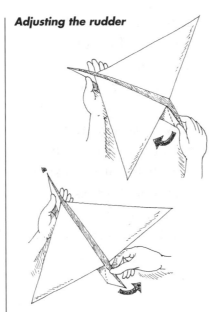

go left, bend the rudder to the left.

THROWING THE PLANES

Now that you have your elevators and rudder adjusted, you're

ready to send your plane soaring. A good flight requires a good throw. The first thing to do is get a good grip on your plane. For most planes, your best bet is to pinch the body (fuselage) toward the front, using your thumb and pointer finger. (The Robo-Chopper, Dragon Ring, and Glider all use different throws; they're described in the folding

How to throw most paper airplanes

PILOT'S ALPHABET

Pilots use words rather than letters when identifying their aircraft over the radio, because it's easier to understand "Orlando Tower, this is Cessna 7-3-4 Sierra Foxtrot" than "This is Cessna 7-3-4-S-F," since "S" and "F" sounds alike. Here's the full pilots' alphabet.

A - Alfa	N - November
B - Bravo	O - Oscar
C - Charlie	P - Papa
D - Delta	Q - Quebec
E - Echo	R - Romeo
F - Foxtrot	S - Sierra
G - Golf	T - Tango
H - Hotel	U - Uniform
I -India	V - Victor
J - Juliet	W- Whiskey
K - Kilo	X - X-ray
L - Lima	Y - Yankee
M- Mike	Z - Zulu

sections for those planes.)

The kind of throw you use depends on how you've adjusted your plane. If your plane is set to fly slowly (if you've added up elevator), hold the plane just in front of your shoulder and gently toss it forward and slightly downward. If your plane is set to fly fast (you haven't added much up elevator), also hold the plane in front of your shoulder but throw it quickly forward. Be sure to aim a little past your target.

THE WORLD RECORD THROW

The key to getting a paper airplane to fly for a long time is to get it high in the air—at least 50 feet high for a world record—so it has time to float down slowly. The way to get a paper airplane 50 feet in the air is to throw it straight up at 60 miles an hour. This requires a strong arm. I developed my throw by working out with weights and using what I had learned in a class on biomechanics, the science of how the body works like a machine. My throw is a combination of a baseball throw and a shot-put throw, with a few other movements thrown in. It's not a natural throw at first, but you can get used to it.

The World Record Throw

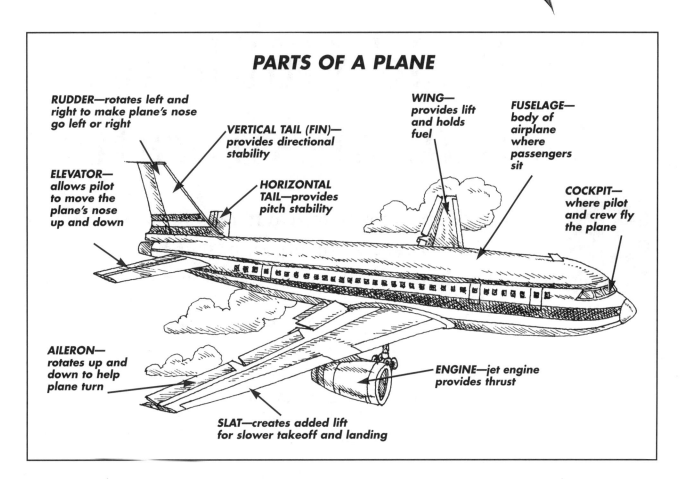

PARTS OF A PLANE

RUDDER—rotates left and right to make plane's nose go left or right

VERTICAL TAIL (FIN)—provides directional stability

ELEVATOR—allows pilot to move the plane's nose up and down

HORIZONTAL TAIL—provides pitch stability

WING—provides lift and holds fuel

FUSELAGE—body of airplane where passengers sit

COCKPIT—where pilot and crew fly the plane

AILERON—rotates up and down to help plane turn

ENGINE—jet engine provides thrust

SLAT—creates added lift for slower takeoff and landing

GIVE IT A TRY To attempt a world record throw, you need a large room with a very high ceiling (such as a gym or auditorium) and a World Record Paper Airplane. It's also handy to have a stopwatch and a pencil and paper to record your times.

Throw your plane normally a few times, adjusting it as needed to make sure it's flying slowly and straight. When it flies well, begin throwing a little harder and a little more upward. Don't be afraid to try different adjustments to the elevators or rudder to make it fly better.

When you're happy with its flight, throw your airplane as close to straight up as you can. You can try to throw it like I do by following the pictures on page 14. If you find this difficult, don't worry; just throw your plane as high in the air as you can. My throw, which I developed over many years, is the best way for me to throw planes. You may develop your own

throwing technique.

If you have a stopwatch, write down your best times and compare them with your friends' flight times.

FAST FACT

Air gets colder as you go higher. On a summer day it is about 40 degrees below zero at 32,000 feet (about six miles above ground), where most airlines fly.

A Field Guide to Common Aircraft

 It's fun to be able to recognize different airplanes, whether you see them parked at an airport or flying in the sky. Here are eight of the most often seen aircraft and ways to recognize them.

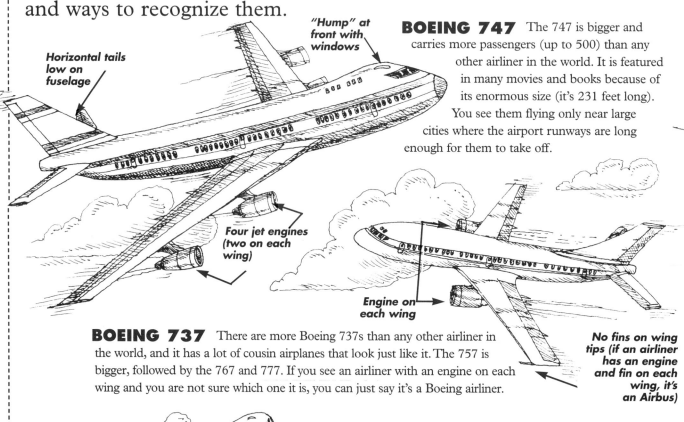

"Hump" at front with windows

Horizontal tails low on fuselage

BOEING 747 The 747 is bigger and carries more passengers (up to 500) than any other airliner in the world. It is featured in many movies and books because of its enormous size (it's 231 feet long). You see them flying only near large cities where the airport runways are long enough for them to take off.

Four jet engines (two on each wing)

Engine on each wing

BOEING 737 There are more Boeing 737s than any other airliner in the world, and it has a lot of cousin airplanes that look just like it. The 757 is bigger, followed by the 767 and 777. If you see an airliner with an engine on each wing and you are not sure which one it is, you can just say it's a Boeing airliner.

No fins on wing tips (if an airliner has an engine and fin on each wing, it's an Airbus)

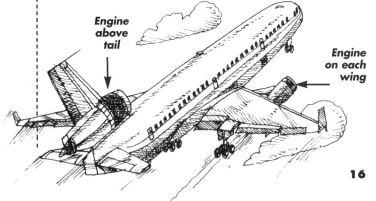

Engine above tail

Engine on each wing

MCDONNELL DOUGLAS MD-11
The MD-11 is an upgrade of the DC-10 (the DC-10 does not have fins on its wing tips). The most distinctive feature of this plane is its three engines. Because the MD-11 is large (about three-quarters the size of the 747), it is normally seen only near large airports that are able to handle such a big plane.

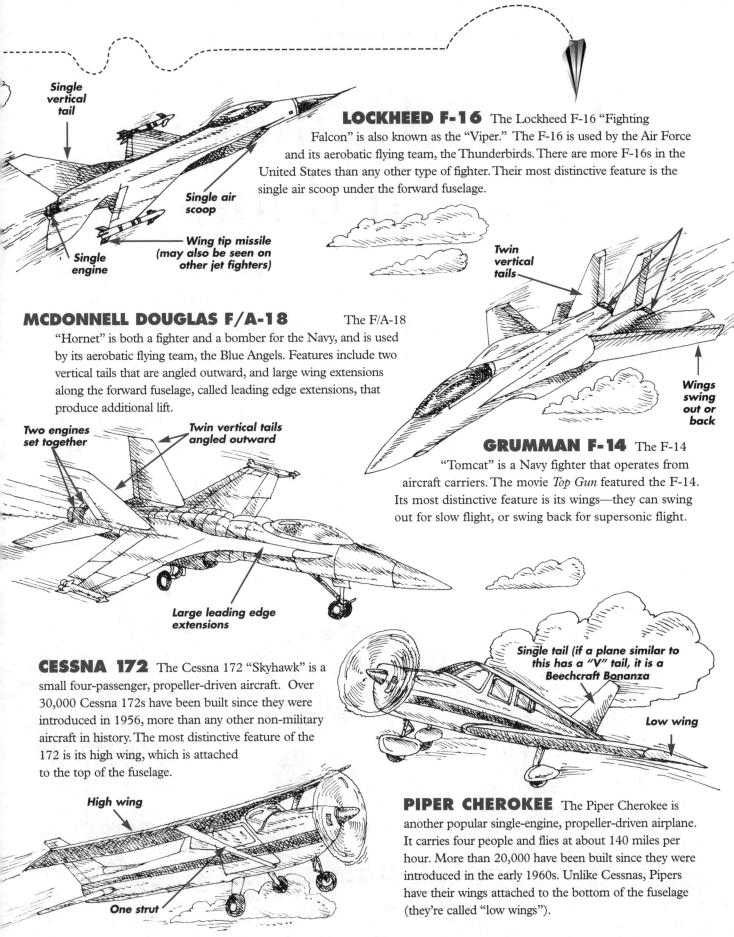

Single vertical tail

Single air scoop

Single engine

Wing tip missile (may also be seen on other jet fighters)

LOCKHEED F-16
The Lockheed F-16 "Fighting Falcon" is also known as the "Viper." The F-16 is used by the Air Force and its aerobatic flying team, the Thunderbirds. There are more F-16s in the United States than any other type of fighter. Their most distinctive feature is the single air scoop under the forward fuselage.

MCDONNELL DOUGLAS F/A-18
The F/A-18 "Hornet" is both a fighter and a bomber for the Navy, and is used by its aerobatic flying team, the Blue Angels. Features include two vertical tails that are angled outward, and large wing extensions along the forward fuselage, called leading edge extensions, that produce additional lift.

Two engines set together

Twin vertical tails angled outward

Large leading edge extensions

Twin vertical tails

Wings swing out or back

GRUMMAN F-14
The F-14 "Tomcat" is a Navy fighter that operates from aircraft carriers. The movie *Top Gun* featured the F-14. Its most distinctive feature is its wings—they can swing out for slow flight, or swing back for supersonic flight.

CESSNA 172
The Cessna 172 "Skyhawk" is a small four-passenger, propeller-driven aircraft. Over 30,000 Cessna 172s have been built since they were introduced in 1956, more than any other non-military aircraft in history. The most distinctive feature of the 172 is its high wing, which is attached to the top of the fuselage.

High wing

One strut

Single tail (if a plane similar to this has a "V" tail, it is a Beechcraft Bonanza

Low wing

PIPER CHEROKEE
The Piper Cherokee is another popular single-engine, propeller-driven airplane. It carries four people and flies at about 140 miles per hour. More than 20,000 have been built since they were introduced in the early 1960s. Unlike Cessnas, Pipers have their wings attached to the bottom of the fuselage (they're called "low wings").

Great Games to Play Indoors

A lot of the paper airplane flying you do will be indoors, at home. Indoor flying has some major advantages— no wind to carry off your plane or send it crashing to the ground. No rain to turn it into a soggy wreck. No sun to get in your eyes. No trees or bushes to gobble up your airplane in their branches. And indoors is great for paper airplane contests because it means everyone flies under the same conditions. (For more on paper airplane contests, see pages 26-28.)

But indoor flying also has a few problems, namely walls and ceilings, not to mention furniture, to crash into. The thing to do is to turn these drawbacks into benefits. Here are some games you can play that take advantage of the fact that you're inside.

Catching a plane

BE A PAPER AIRPLANE ENGINEER

Once you've folded and flown a lot of the planes in this book, you'll have a feel for what a paper airplane needs to fly well, and you can begin designing your own models.

You may want to start by changing some of our designs—adding wing tips or a fin, or making the body of the plane longer or shorter. Once you feel good about your modifications, create your own original designs.

Get a big stack of paper and experiment with different folds and cuts. Don't worry if a lot of your planes don't fly at all well. You may have to make a lot of duds before you hit on a great new design. Remember that paper airplanes need weight and strength in the nose, so you'll probably want to have plenty of folds toward the front of the plane.

Regular 8½-by-11-inch typing or copier paper is good for most paper airplane designs, but you can try out other types of paper, too. Experiment with coloring your planes in different ways—with felt-tipped markers, stickers, or paint.

CATCHING A PLANE

You'll need two or more people and at least one airplane for this game. Any model will do, but we recommend the Butterfly, Slice, or Count. Start by standing close together, then have each player take two big steps away from the others. Throw the plane back and forth as if it were a ball, with the players plucking it from the air. Try to grab the plane by the fuselage so it doesn't get squished. After you've successfully thrown and caught the plane a few times, each player should take another step back. Keep throwing and stepping back until the distance between you is too great, or you bump into a wall or piece of furniture.

Variation: Once you get good at the game, try using as many planes as there are players so that everybody is throwing and catching at the same time.

TARGET PRACTICE

Pick a target, any target (but not your little brother or the dog). It could be an armchair, the runway on the airport poster in this book, or if you want to pretend you're a fighter-jet pilot landing on an aircraft carrier, the end of a table or ironing board. Good planes to use are the Slice, Great White, or Thunderbolt. Stand back about 10 feet from the target and take aim. Once you've landed in the right place three times, take a big step back and try again. Keep throwing and stepping back until you're out of range.

This is a great game to play by yourself, but it's also fun with friends. Keep score by giving each player a point every time he or she hits the target; whoever has the highest number of points after a certain number of throws, say 20, wins.

PAPER AIRPLANE GOLF

This game is a lot like the real game of golf, but you play it indoors using your arm and a paper airplane rather than outside using golf clubs and a ball, and it doesn't take nearly as long. You can play the game alone or with friends. We recommend using the Count, Slice, or Butterfly.

Choose between three and nine landing spots (these will be your "holes"), such as chairs, tables, and small rugs. They don't all have to be within one throw of each other; in fact they don't

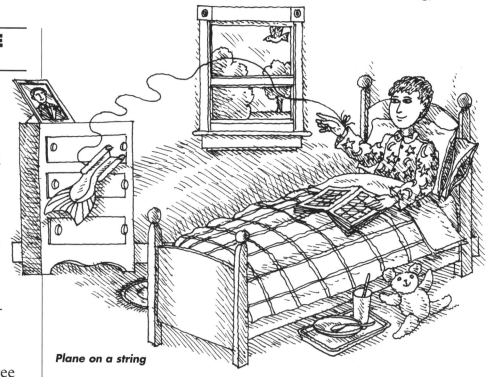

Plane on a string

FAST FACT

The longest recorded distance flown by a paper airplane thrown from the ground indoors is 193 feet (more than twice the length of a basketball court). It was thrown by Tony Feltch in La Crosse, Wisconsin, on May 21, 1985.

even have to be in the same room. In golf it's normal to have to hit a few shots between holes, and in this game you can set it up so that some holes require at least three to five throws. If you want, number the "holes" with pieces of paper so you remember the order you're supposed to go in. The object of the game is to land on all the spots using the fewest number of throws. If you set up a challenging and fun course, write down where all the holes are so you can play the course again and improve your "golf" game.

PLANE ON A STRING

This is an excellent game to play if you're sick and have to stay in bed. It's also fun if you're feeling lazy or watching TV. All you need is a paper airplane (almost any kind will do), about 15 feet of string or strong thread, and some tape. Tape the string to the plane near where you'd hold it to throw it. Then tie the other end of the string to your wrist. Choose or set up a target about 10 feet away from where you are and see how well you can land on it.

Fearless Outdoor Flying

The biggest difference between indoor and outdoor flying is the weather. Obviously rain and darkness are enemies of the outdoor paper airplane pilot. But wind can be a good friend. It can carry your plane a long distance and keep it in the air for a long time.

If you want your plane to fly a long distance, stand with the wind blowing on your back and gently throw your plane forward (in the direction the wind is blowing). Like a real airplane pilot, you'll be taking advantage of **tailwinds** to fly your plane a long way without using much energy.

To take advantage of **headwinds,** throw your plane directly into the wind (so the wind is blowing in your face). Throwing into the wind is like getting a really fast throw for free. The extra air speed over the wings (extra lift) makes the plane climb high. Your plane will stay in the air for a long time but won't fly very far because the wind will be against it.

Special air currents called **thermals** can also help paper airplanes soar high in the sky for a long time. Thermals are channels of warm rising air, and if your paper airplane flies into one, it will fly skyward with the rising air. Thermals are mostly found on sunny days over open dry ground. Blacktop parking lots are good places to find thermals, because as the pavement heats up, it creates thermals.

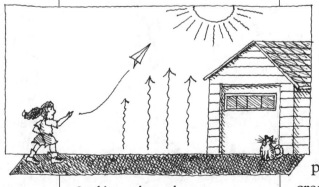

Catching a thermal

If you feel the wind suddenly shift, it could mean a thermal has started nearby. Throw your plane as high as possible in the direction of the wind shift. Be prepared to throw your plane quickly; thermals usually don't last very long. And don't get frustrated if your plane doesn't climb up and out of sight on your first few throws. Thermals can be tricky to catch.

The great outdoors offers a lot of possibilities for games that take advantage of the space available or the wind. Here are three of my favorites.

LONG DISTANCE FLIGHTS

How far can you fly a paper airplane? First, make a plane—I recommend the Count or the Slice. Find an open area like a field or a playground, and choose a starting spot. Figure out which way the wind is blowing by tossing some grass or a scrap of paper in the air. The direction the wind blows the grass or scrap is the direction you want to throw your plane. Give your plane a hard throw and see how far it flies. Return to the starting spot to see if you can do better, or challenge your friends to fly their planes as far as you did.

PAPER AIRPLANE RACE

Find a building you can run around, and challenge some friends to a race. Have everyone fold a

paper airplane—the Count and the Slice are good bets. The goal is to see who can fly his or her plane around the building the quickest. Have everyone stand together at a starting line and throw their planes at the same time. Run to your plane, pick it up, and throw it again. Keep throwing and running until you get around the building. The first person whose plane flies over the starting line is the winner!

SOLO CATCH

An activity I really enjoy is throwing a paper airplane high into the air and trying to catch it before it lands. The World Record and Butterfly airplanes are best for this. First, adjust your plane to fly slowly by adding a little up elevator. Next, face into the wind and throw your airplane as high as you can. As your plane circles down, run toward it and try to catch it before it hits the ground. Be sure to catch it gently. You don't want to turn your paper airplane into a paper ball.

How to Be a Stunt Pilot

 Once you feel comfortable flying your planes (adjusting and throwing them to fly the way you want—fast or slow, left or right), you may want to try your hand at stunts. Performing stunts (also known as aerobatics) requires specific adjustments and throws. Nothing complicated—it's just the results that look fancy. The Aerobat is a good bet for all stunts, but you can also use the Pirate's Secret or the World Record Paper Airplane.

LOOPS

Loops have thrilled pilots and spectators since the first loop was performed in a real plane in 1913. Just about anyone can make a paper airplane loop—fly up, then down and around in a circle. It helps to have a high ceiling or to be outside, but it's not necessary.

WHAT TO DO Test fly your plane and adjust it to fly straight. Then add a lot of up elevator—much more than you usually would. Bend the elevators almost straight up.

Hold your plane a little behind your shoulder and give it a gentle toss straight up. Your plane should climb two or three feet, stop, flip over backward, dive at the ground, then pull up before hitting the floor. It may take some practice to get your throw just right, but the results will be worth it.

> ### FAST FACT
>
> The record for consecutive loops performed by a real airplane is 2,368—talk about getting dizzy! It was set in 1986 by David Childs in a Belanca Decathlon, a propeller-driven aerobatic airplane.

DIVES

A dive is when a plane is zooming straight for the ground, but pulls itself up at the last moment. Paper airplanes are amazing because they can do this even if they aren't thrown from very high and are one second away from crashing.

WHAT TO DO Start by adding a lot of up elevator to your plane. Then hold it as high above your head as you can and a little bit in front of you. If you are not very tall, stand on a sturdy stool or chair. Point the nose straight down and drop the plane. It should swoop to the ground, then pull out of the dive before it hits the floor.

TAILSLIDES

A tailslide is a sort of backward dive—the plane's nose is pointed straight up, but the plane is flying backward toward the ground. The plane will seemingly be headed for a crash, then flip over, dive, and pull itself up.

WHAT TO DO As for a dive, hold your plane as high above your head as you can and slightly in front of you. You may want to stand on a sturdy chair or stool. The plane's nose should be pointed up. Drop the plane and

watch how it starts out flying backward, then turns over and pulls itself up.

CIRCLES

Have you ever seen someone throw a boomerang? It flies off, then comes back to the thrower so he or she can catch it. Well, with practice and patience you can make a paper airplane do a similar thing—fly around in a circle, so it returns to you.

WHAT TO DO Test fly your plane and adjust it to fly straight. Then add a lot of up elevator. The amount of up elevator you add will probably make the plane bob up and down when flown straight, but it's needed to make the plane turn well.

If you're right-handed, it's easiest to make your plane turn in a circle to the right. Hold the plane in front of you at shoulder height, with the plane's right wing lower than its left (the plane will be *banked* right). If you're left-handed, you'll want to make your plane circle to the left. Hold the plane so it's banked left. Throw the plane straight ahead (the fact that you've banked the wings will make the plane turn). Your goal is to make a level flight. If you throw it too hard, it will climb; if you throw it too softly, it will dive. Keep throwing until you're comfortable getting your plane to make a level turn.

If your plane doesn't make a full circle, bend the rudder to help it along. If you're throwing with your right hand, bend the rudder to the right. If you're left-handed, bend the rudder to the left.

Eventually, you'll be able to get your plane to make full circles so that it returns to you and, without having to take a step, you can reach out and catch it.

MAKING A PAPER AIRPLANE MOBILE

What better way to keep your paper airplanes flying all the time than by making them into a paper airplane mobile? Here's one that's quick and easy to make.

WHAT YOU NEED:
- 3 wire hangers
- Twist-ties (the kind that come with food storage or garbage bags)
- Tape
- String or strong thread
- 5 of your favorite paper airplanes

1. Find a place to hang one of the hangers so that you have room to work with it. This could be an empty area in a closet, but if that's too high for comfort or you don't want to work standing up, you could place a broom across the top of two chairs and hang the hanger between them.

2. Hang the other two hangers from each of the first hanger's corners. Wrap a twist-tie around each of the lower hangers where it joins the top hanger to keep the lower hangers from sliding around.

3. Find or fold five paper airplanes. I prefer to use "used" paper airplanes. That way I can recycle the paper airplanes that have had a few too many rough landings.

4. Cut five 20- to 30-inch lengths of string or thread and fold each one in half. Take one of your chosen planes and try to find its balance point—the place where the front and back each weigh the same. Tape the looped end of the string or thread to that point. Even if you've found the balance point with your fingers, you will likely need to move the tape around a little to find the exact balance point—otherwise the plane's nose will pitch up or down.

5. Tie a plane to each corner of the two lower hangers. You can make your strings different lengths or all the same—whatever looks best to you—as long as the hangers remain balanced. Tie the fifth plane to the center of the top hanger so that it's a different length from the other planes. Wrap a twist-tie or a piece of tape around the hanger where each plane is tied to keep them from sliding around on the hanger. Ask a grown-up to help you find a good place to hang your mobile. When the wind blows, your planes will take off!

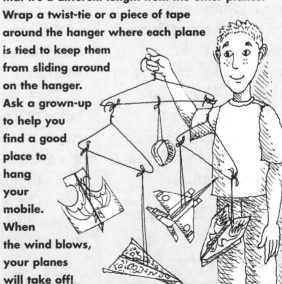

Setting Up a Paper Airplane Contest

When you're flying paper airplanes with friends, it's only natural that you'll want to see who has the best plane and who is the best flier. What starts out as casual throwing can easily turn into an informal paper airplane contest. Contests are fun because they not only challenge you to do your best, but also compare your skills with your friends', which can help you improve your techniques. They're easy to organize, and can be as formal or informal as you want.

Here are guidelines for setting up two different types of contests—distance and time aloft. You need only two people for a contest, but it's fun to have more. I think three to six is ideal. That means there are enough people for a good competition, but not so many that the event gets confusing.

DISTANCE CONTESTS

The challenge here is to see who can throw his or her plane the farthest. Ideally you can set up your contest in a large indoor space—that way no one has the advantage or disadvantage of a sudden wind gust.

How far is a good distance flight? Twenty feet is respectable, and thirty feet is a great throw. Fifty feet will win most adult contests. The world record for indoor flight is almost 200 feet. Good luck!

WHAT YOU NEED Masking tape or rope, paper airplanes, small prizes such as penny candy or stickers (optional).

WHAT TO DO Find a place to have your contest and choose a starting

line. Mark it with masking tape (or, if you're outdoors, a piece of rope). Gymnasiums are great places for distance contests, as are long hallways and big rooms. If you can't find a big enough indoor space, outside is OK, too. Just choose a day that's not too windy.

Fold your planes. You can ask everybody to use the same model or let people choose their own. Make sure everyone puts his or her name on the plane.

Let everybody make a few practice throws. Then, when everyone is ready, have each participant stand behind the starting line and make an official throw. Leave all the planes where they land until everyone has thrown. The one farthest from the starting line is the winner.

If you have time for another round or two, ask each person to mark where his or her plane landed with a piece of tape (or a stone or twig, if you're outdoors), and throw again. See if all the contestants can improve their flights.

TIPS FOR WINNING Use a pointed-nose plane like the Slice or the Count. Small adjustments are the secret to making a good paper airplane into a great one. Make several short throws and, after each one, adjust your plane to improve its flight. Try to make it fly straight (bend the rudder as needed) and fast (you will need very little up elevator). If the contest rules allow it, add a paper clip to the nose of

your plane. Your best-bet distance throw is one that's hard and angled a little up.

TIME ALOFT CONTESTS

This is my favorite kind of contest. The goal is to keep your plane in the air for the greatest amount of time. You will need a plane that floats well and you should know how to fine-tune and adjust it. It's a test of both your paper airplane–making skills and your flying ability.

How many seconds is a long flight? Five seconds doesn't sound long, but is a good flight. Ten seconds is very difficult—consider yourself an expert if you can get near that. I had to train with weights and practice for years to achieve my world record flight of 18.8 seconds.

WHAT YOU NEED Stopwatch, pencil or pen and paper, paper airplanes, small prizes such as penny candy or stickers (optional).

WHAT TO DO Find a place to have your contest. You need a big room with tall ceilings—a gymnasium would be good—if you're going to have it inside, or a big open area if you're going to be outside. As in distance contests, indoors is better—it means that no one faces an advantage or disadvantage from the wind or thermals. But a large enough indoor space can be hard to find, so you'll likely have to make do with outside. Choose a day that's calm.

Gather supplies that you need and get all your contestants together. They can make their planes on the spot, or you can ask them to bring their planes already folded. Decide in advance if they can use any plane they want or must all use the same model. Let everyone make several practice throws and give each time to adjust their planes.

Choose one person to be the timer and another to be the judge for all but their own throws (someone else can time and record their throws). The timer uses the stopwatch to time each flight, and the judge writes down the name of the contestant and the number of seconds the timer calls out. The timer should start the stopwatch as soon as the thrower lets go of the plane and stop it as soon as the plane lands (or hits something). The judge tells each person when he or she can make a throw.

Have everyone make one official throw. The person with the longest-lasting flight wins the round. It's fun to have a few rounds. If, after a few rounds, two people tie for first place or have very close times, you can have a runoff between them. The person with the longest flight of the day wins the contest.

TIPS FOR WINNING
Not surprisingly, I think the World Record Paper Airplane is the best plane to use, but the Pirate's Secret, the Aerobat, and the Count stay aloft well, too. Fly them all before the contest and see which works best for you. Adjust your plane to fly slowly—use quite a bit of up elevator, but not so much that it makes the plane "porpoise" up and down. Throw your plane hard and up. Some planes do best if you throw them straight up; others work better if you bank them (tilt their wings to one side) and throw them not quite straight up.

The Association of Paper Airplane Pilots

hereby awards

this

Paper Airplane Pilot's License

The license acknowledges the recipient's superior skills in folding, adjusting, and flying paper airplanes and grants the authority to offer advice and aid to less experienced paper airplane pilots, even those of a more advanced age.

Ken D. Blackburn

World Record Holder

Jeff Lamm

President

OFFICIAL APAP SEAL OF AERONAUTIC EXCELLENCE

Paper Airplane Pilot's Checklist

BEFORE TAKEOFF, MAKE SURE OF THE FOLLOWING:

1. Wings are same size and shape and are not warped. Wings form a slight "Y" shape with body of plane.

2. Plane's elevators have been adjusted for fast or slow flight, as desired.

3. Plane's rudder has been adjusted for straight or turning flight, as desired.

4. Pilot's throwing arm is in good shape, ready to make a smooth, steady throw.

5. If pilot has added a paper clip to the plane's nose, check to see that it's properly attached. After a few landings, they tend to slip.

6. Flying conditions are acceptable—the flying area is cleared of all nonparticipating people and animals and the weather is appropriate for the desired flight. If outdoors, determine wind direction.

How to Fold, Fix, and Fly the Planes in this Book

THE Count

The Count is a ghoulishly good glider. It's a type of dart, but has more paper in the nose. This gives it extra stability, making it ideal for long, straight flights. It's also good for precision flying. With a little practice, you can use it to make pinpoint landings. The Count flies best if you add a little up elevator, but be careful not to add too much—this plane is very sensitive to elevator adjustments. And remember not to let the vampire out after the sun goes down!

WHAT TO DO IF...

YOUR PLANE DIVES AND CRASHES: Add up elevator by bending the back edges of the wings up a little. Or throw the plane a little harder. **NOTE:** The Count is very sensitive to up elevator, so only a little is needed for slow flight.

YOUR PLANE CLIMBS, SLOWS, THEN CRASHES: Reduce the amount of up elevator by making the back edges of the wings flatter. Or throw the plane a little slower.

YOUR PLANE HEADS OFF TO THE RIGHT: Bend the rudder a little to the left.

YOUR PLANE HEADS OFF TO THE LEFT: Bend the rudder a little to the right.

elevator

rudder   *elevator*

Making the Count

Don't forget: Fold in on the dashed red lines (so you can't see them anymore) and fold away on the dotted yellow lines (you'll still be able to see them along the outside of the creases).

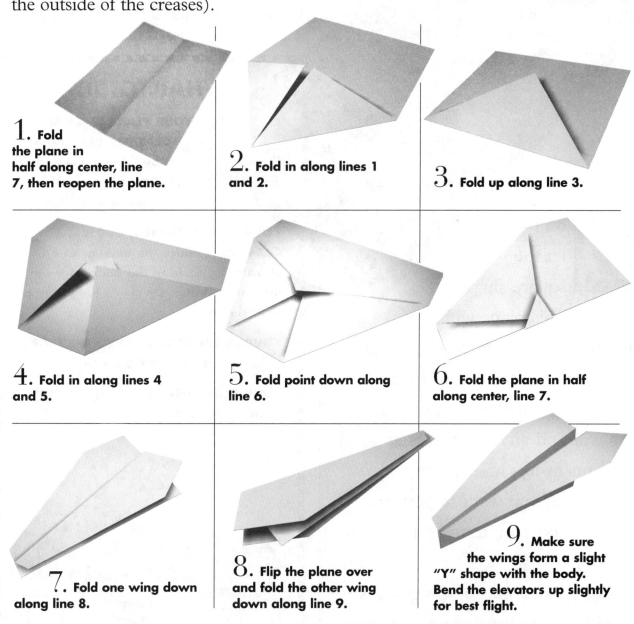

1. Fold the plane in half along center, line 7, then reopen the plane.

2. Fold in along lines 1 and 2.

3. Fold up along line 3.

4. Fold in along lines 4 and 5.

5. Fold point down along line 6.

6. Fold the plane in half along center, line 7.

7. Fold one wing down along line 8.

8. Flip the plane over and fold the other wing down along line 9.

9. Make sure the wings form a slight "Y" shape with the body. Bend the elevators up slightly for best flight.

Pirate's Secret

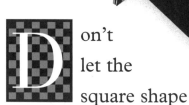

Write a private note to a friend at the X on the back, then fold the plane up and send it on its way.

D on't let the square shape fool you; this plane will out-glide most pointed-nose paper planes and is just as fast. In fact, it's one of the best-flying paper planes you will find anywhere. It is as good at stunts as it is at distance and accuracy. If you want to perform stunts, make sure to use a lot of up elevator.

But the best part of this plane is that it's an excellent secret messenger.

WHAT TO DO IF...

YOUR PLANE DIVES AND CRASHES: Add up elevator by bending the back edges of the wings up a little. Or throw the plane a little harder.

YOUR PLANE CLIMBS, SLOWS, THEN CRASHES: Reduce the amount of up elevator by making the back edges of the wings flatter. Or throw the plane a little slower.

YOUR PLANE HEADS OFF TO THE RIGHT: Bend the rudder a little to the left.

YOUR PLANE HEADS OFF TO THE LEFT: Bend the rudder a little to the right.

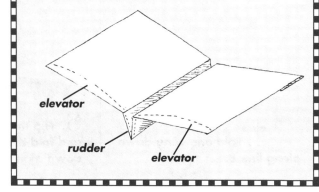

elevator

rudder   elevator

Making the Pirate's Secret

Don't forget: Fold in on the dashed purple lines (so you can't see them anymore) and fold away on the dotted yellow lines (you'll still be able to see them along the outside of the creases). **Folding tip:** This model can get a little bulky in the nose (making it hard to fold the wings down), so make your creases as sharp as possible.

1. Fold up along line 1 to line 2.

2. Fold along line 2 to line 3.

3. Fold along line 3 to line 4, and continue folding through line 8.

4. Flip plane over and fold in half along line 9.

5. Fold one wing up along line 10.

6. Flip plane over and fold the other wing down along line 11.

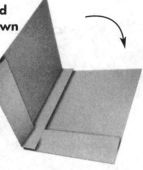

7. Make sure the wings form a slight "Y" shape with the body. Bend the elevators up slightly for best flight.

THE Slice

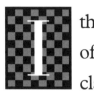 think you will like the flavor of this paper airplane. It's a classic dart (you've probably made something similar before). It is easy to fold, looks good, and flies well, too (especially if you add a little up elevator). It's excellent for long-distance flights and flights requiring accuracy. Try slipping a paper clip over the nose to create an extra-stable fast flier. And don't let anyone take a bite out of your plane!

WHAT TO DO IF...

YOUR PLANE DIVES AND CRASHES: Add up elevator by bending the back edges of the wings up a little. Or throw the plane a little harder.

YOUR PLANE CLIMBS, SLOWS, THEN CRASHES: Reduce the amount of up elevator by making the back edges of the wings flatter. Or throw the plane a little slower.

YOUR PLANE HEADS OFF TO THE RIGHT: Bend the rudder a little to the left.

YOUR PLANE HEADS OFF TO THE LEFT: Bend the rudder a little to the right.

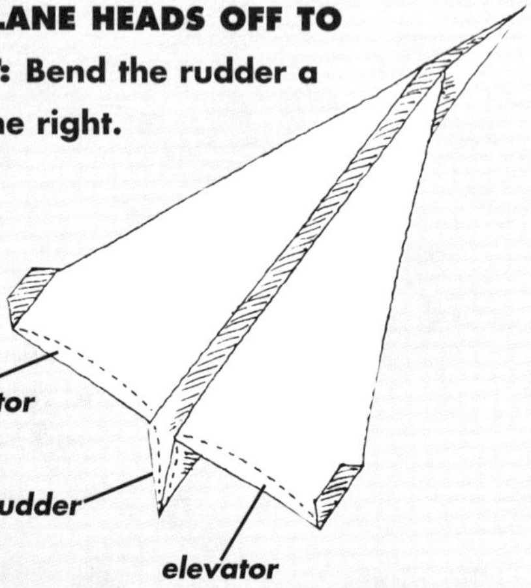

elevator

rudder

elevator

Making the Slice

Don't forget: Fold in on the dashed blue lines (so you can't see them anymore) and fold away on the dotted yellow lines (you'll still be able to see them along the outside of the creases).

1. **Fold plane in half along center, line 5, and reopen.**

2. **Fold in along lines 1 and 2.**

3. **Fold in along lines 3 and 4.**

4. **Fold plane in half along center, line 5.**

5. **Fold one wing down along line 6.**

6. **Flip plane over and fold the other wing up along line 7.**

7. **Open plane and fold wing tips up along lines 8 and 9. Make sure the wings form a slight "Y" shape with the body. Bend the elevators up slightly for best flight.**

THE Glider

 ike real gliders, this paper airplane has long, skinny wings. Real gliders, which are airplanes without engines, use such wings because these reduce drag and offer better performance. These aircraft are towed into the sky by a plane with an engine, then take advantage of air currents to stay aloft for hours. Your glider is also capable of long floating flights.

NOTE: Because the Glider doesn't have a body to grasp, it requires a different throw. Hold the plane with the folded edge facing forward, your pointer finger on top, and your thumb and middle finger below (see picture). Gently push the plane forward.

WHAT TO DO IF...

YOUR PLANE DIVES AND CRASHES: Add up elevator by bending the back edges of the wings up a little. Or throw the plane a little harder.

YOUR PLANE CLIMBS, SLOWS, THEN CRASHES: Reduce the amount of up elevator by making the back edges of the wings flatter. Or throw the plane a little slower.

YOUR PLANE HEADS OFF TO THE RIGHT: Bend the left elevator up a little.

YOUR PLANE HEADS OFF TO THE LEFT: Bend the right elevator up a little.

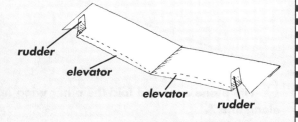

rudder

elevator

elevator

rudder

Making the Glider

Don't forget: Cut along the solid white lines. Fold in on the dashed yellow lines (so you can't see them anymore) and fold away on the dotted red lines (you'll still be able to see them along the outside of the creases).

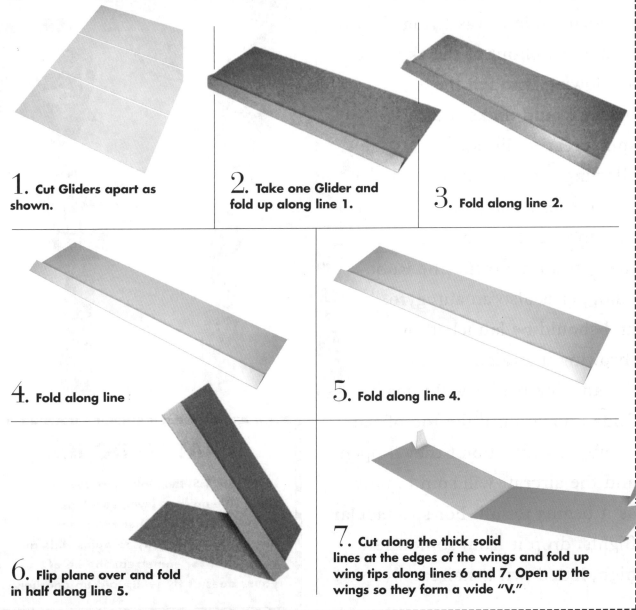

1. Cut Gliders apart as shown.

2. Take one Glider and fold up along line 1.

3. Fold along line 2.

4. Fold along line

5. Fold along line 4.

6. Flip plane over and fold in half along line 5.

7. Cut along the thick solid lines at the edges of the wings and fold up wing tips along lines 6 and 7. Open up the wings so they form a wide "V."

Robo-Chopper

Did you ever wonder what would happen to a helicopter if the engine stopped while it was flying? No, it wouldn't fall out of the sky. The air flowing through the blades would make them spin, creating lift and allowing the aircraft to become an autogyro, descending slowly rather than crashing down. The Robo-Chopper is also an autogyro, and should be launched by throwing it straight up into the air. The blades will remain folded down until the top of the climb, at which point they'll open and the aircraft will spin rapidly as it begins to fall. For spectacular flights, drop it from somewhere high, like down a staircase.

WHAT TO DO IF...

IT DOESN'T SPIN: Make sure the blades are a little up from level, so it looks like a "Y" from the side. Other than that, there's really no way to adjust this aircraft, so if for some reason one of yours doesn't fly well, fold up another.

Making the Robo-Chopper

Don't forget: Cut along the solid white lines. Fold in on the dashed black lines (so you can't see them anymore) and fold away on the dotted gray lines (you'll still be able to see them along the outside of the creases).

1. Cut Robo-Choppers apart as shown.

2. Take one Chopper and cut along solid white lines as shown.

3. Fold down on lines 1 and 2.

4. Fold in along line 3.

5. Fold in along line 4.

6. Fold up along line 5. If you want, tape fold in place.

7. Fold the blades down along lines 6 and 7 as shown.

Aerobat

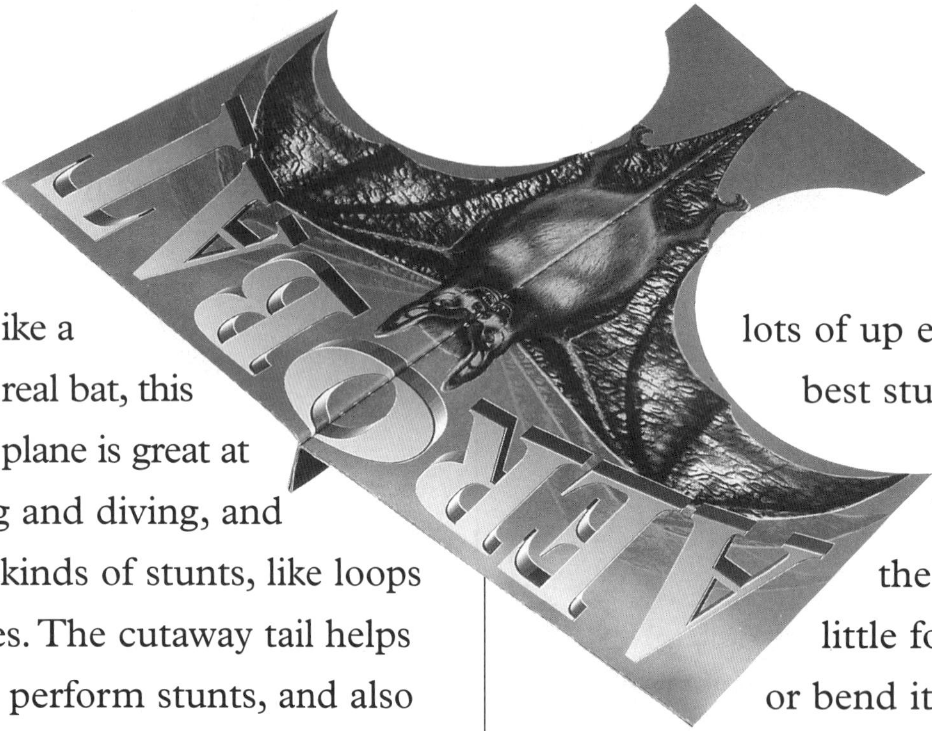

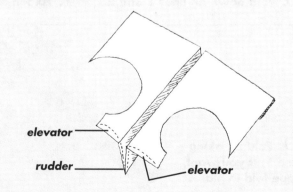

Like a real bat, this plane is great at swooping and diving, and doing all kinds of stunts, like loops and circles. The cutaway tail helps the plane perform stunts, and also adds stability, making it great for "normal" flying, too. Be sure to use lots of up elevator for best stunt flying. Try bending the rudder a little for turns, or bend it a lot for diving spirals. See if you can invent some new stunts of your own.

WHAT TO DO IF...

YOUR PLANE DIVES AND CRASHES: Add up elevator by bending the back edges of the tails up a little. Or throw the plane a little harder.

YOUR PLANE CLIMBS, SLOWS, THEN CRASHES: Reduce the amount of up elevator by making the back edges of the tails flatter. Or throw the plane a little slower.

YOUR PLANE HEADS OFF TO THE RIGHT: Bend the rudder a little to the left.

YOUR PLANE HEADS OFF TO THE LEFT: Bend the rudder a little to the right.

elevator

rudder — elevator

Making the Aerobat

Don't forget: Cut along the solid white lines. Fold in on the dashed red lines (so you can't see them anymore) and fold away on the dotted green lines (you'll still be able to see them along the outside of the creases).

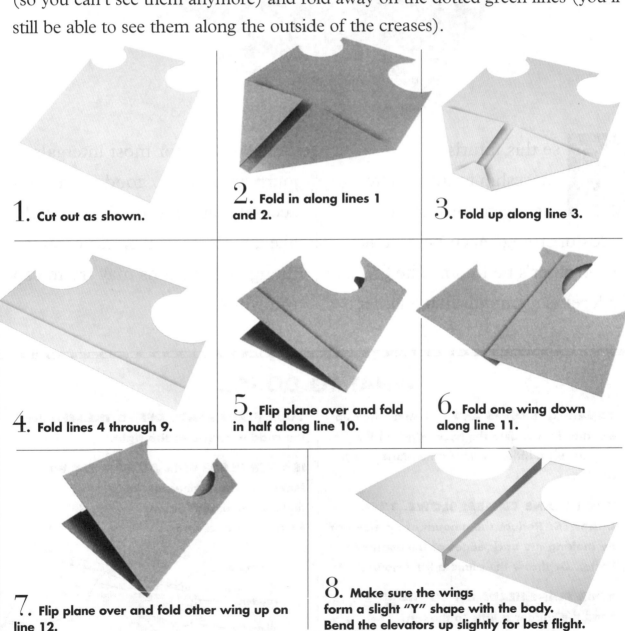

1. Cut out as shown.

2. Fold in along lines 1 and 2.

3. Fold up along line 3.

4. Fold lines 4 through 9.

5. Flip plane over and fold in half along line 10.

6. Fold one wing down along line 11.

7. Flip plane over and fold other wing up on line 12.

8. Make sure the wings form a slight "Y" shape with the body. Bend the elevators up slightly for best flight.

THE S.S. Explorer

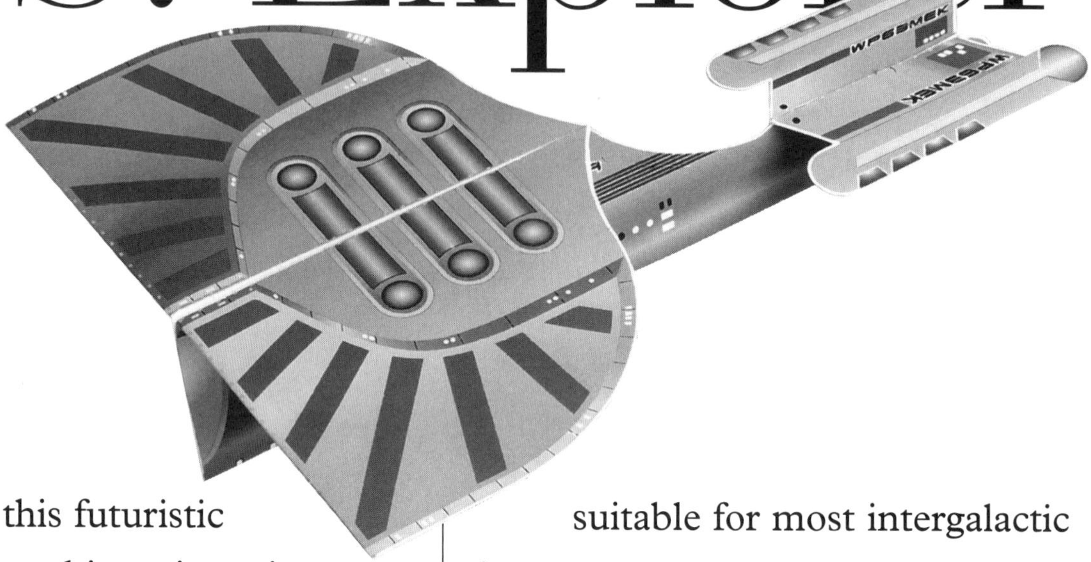

 se this futuristic spaceship to investigate the mysterious home worlds of strange alien beings, like your brother's bedroom. The S.S. Explorer is a smooth-flying glider, suitable for most intergalactic journeys. It's also good for making accurate landings on far-off worlds, like a table or a chair. Be careful though—the aliens may try to capture your ship!

WHAT TO DO IF...

YOUR PLANE DIVES AND CRASHES: Add up elevator by bending the back edges of the engines up a little. Or throw the plane a little harder.

YOUR PLANE CLIMBS, SLOWS, THEN CRASHES: Reduce the amount of up elevator by making the back edges of the engines flatter. Or throw the plane a little slower.

YOUR PLANE HEADS OFF TO THE RIGHT: Bend the rudder a little to the left.

YOUR PLANE HEADS OFF TO THE LEFT: Bend the rudder a little to the right.

IF YOUR PLANE STILL DOESN'T FLY WELL: Make sure the engines are flat and unbent, except for any intentional up elevator.

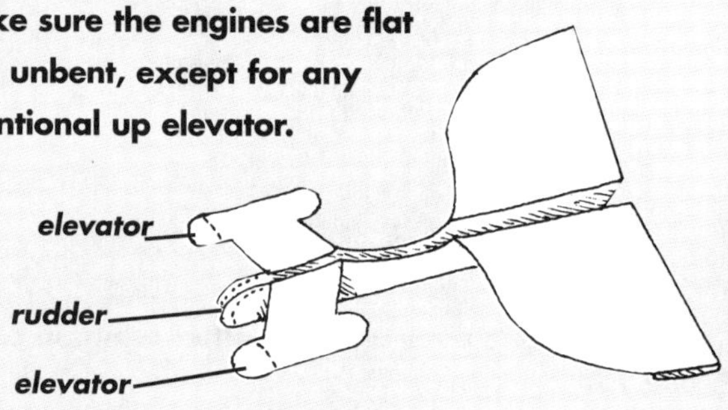

elevator

rudder

elevator

Making the S.S. Explorer

Don't forget: Cut along the solid white lines. Fold in on the dashed yellow lines (so you can't see them anymore) and fold away on the dotted green lines (you'll still be able to see them along the outside of the creases).

1. **Cut out plane as shown. It's easiest to cut out center shape if you fold the plane in half along line 5, then make the cut. Afterward, reopen the plane.**

2. **Fold up along line 1.**

3. **Fold along lines 2, 3, and 4.**

4. **Flip plane over and fold in half along line 5.**

5. **Fold one wing down along line 6 and one engine down along line 7.**

6. **Flip plane over and fold the other wing up along line 8 and the engine up along line 9.**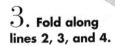

7. **Open up plane so that wings form a slight "Y" shape with the body.**

THE Butterfly

 ature is filled with great fliers—from powerful eagles to soaring swallows to graceful butterflies. You may be thinking, "Butterflies? They're so slow and fragile." But the fact is, some butterflies are amazing fliers. Orange-and-black Monarch butterflies, for instance, travel thousands of miles when they migrate from Mexico to Canada and back each spring and fall. Your Butterfly won't go that far, but it's an excellent flier nonetheless. Leave the elevators flat for fast, direct flight, or use some up elevator to make it float—like a butterfly!

WHAT TO DO IF...

YOUR PLANE DIVES AND CRASHES: Add up elevator by bending the back edges of the tails up a little. Or throw the plane a little harder.

YOUR PLANE CLIMBS, SLOWS, THEN CRASHES: Reduce the amount of up elevator by making the back edges of the tails flatter. Or throw the plane a little slower.

YOUR PLANE HEADS OFF TO THE RIGHT: Bend the rudder a little to the left.

YOUR PLANE HEADS OFF TO THE LEFT: Bend the rudder a little to the right.

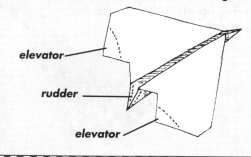

elevator

rudder

elevator

Making the Butterfly

Don't forget: Cut along the solid white lines. Fold in on the dashed pink lines (so you can't see them anymore) and fold away on the dotted yellow lines (you'll still be able to see them along the outside of the creases).

1. Cut tails as shown.

2. Fold in along lines 1 and 2.

3. Fold up along line 3.

4. Fold along lines 4 and 5.

5. Fold the plane in half along line 6.

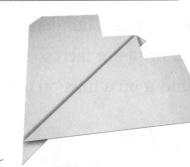

6. Fold one wing down along line 7.

7. Flip plane over and fold the other wing up along line 8.

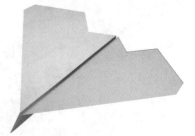

8. Open up plane so that wings form a slight "Y" shape with the body.

THE Thunderbolt

This plane looks good, and flies as good as it looks. The name Thunderbolt is not new to aviation. The P-47 Thunderbold was one of the most rugged and powerful fighters of World War II. The A-10 Thunderbold II served in the Gulf War, with its gun being the largest on any airplane. Your Thunderbold is also a high performance flier, so fold one and send it on a mission down the hall.

WHAT TO DO IF...

YOUR PLANE DIVES AND CRASHES: Add up elevator by bending the back edges of the tails up a little. Or throw the plane a little harder.

YOUR PLANE CLIMBS, SLOWS, THEN CRASHES: Reduce the amount of up elevator by making the back edges of the tails flatter. Or throw the plane a little slower.

YOUR PLANE HEADS OFF TO THE RIGHT: Bend the rudder a little to the left.

YOUR PLANE HEADS OFF TO THE LEFT: Bend the rudder a little to the right.

elevator

rudder

elevator

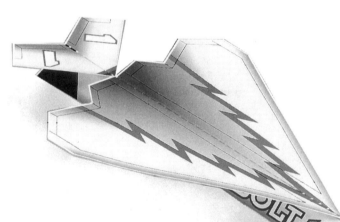

Making the Thunderbolt

Don't forget: Cut along the solid white lines. Fold in on the dashed yellow lines (so you can't see them anymore) and fold away on the dotted pink lines (you'll still be able to see them along the outside of the creases).

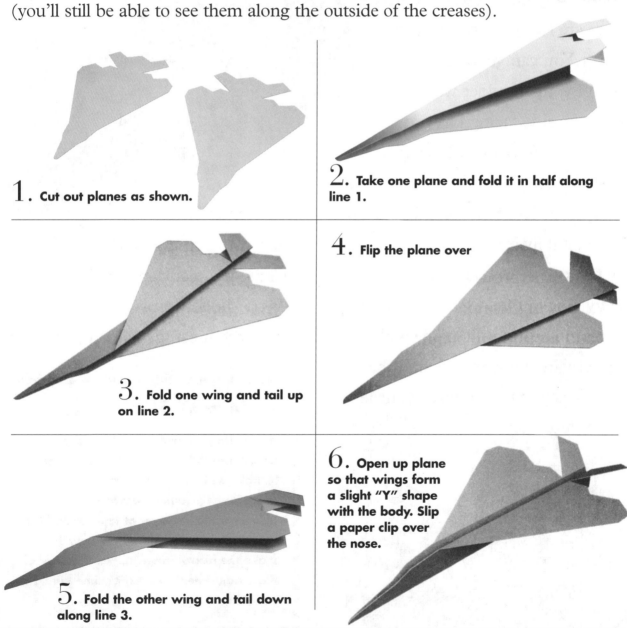

1. Cut out planes as shown.

2. Take one plane and fold it in half along line 1.

3. Fold one wing and tail up on line 2.

4. Flip the plane over

5. Fold the other wing and tail down along line 3.

6. Open up plane so that wings form a slight "Y" shape with the body. Slip a paper clip over the nose.

Dragon Ring

 hat makes this unusual-looking plane fly? A good throw, of course! There are two ways to throw this aircraft. You can gently hold it in front of your shoulder with the folded-up side facing forward (see picture A, below). Now give it a slow push forward. If you can get it to spin by letting it roll off your fingertips, it'll fly even better.

My favorite throw was shown to me by a boy in Georgia. Gently hold your hand around the plane with your arm hanging by your side and the plane facing inward toward your leg

(see picture B). Fling your arm forward, making the plane spin by letting it roll off your fingertips as you throw. See how far you can get your Ring to fly!

WHAT TO DO IF...

If your Dragon Ring won't fly and you're pretty sure that you're throwing it correctly, hold the plane in front of you and make sure it's round, not warped. You can also try adding a layer of tape around the front (where it's folded up), wich will make the aircraft more stable. If neither of these adjustments works, it's time to fold a new Ring.

Making the Dragon Ring

Don't forget: Cut along the solid white lines. Fold in on the dashed blue lines (so you can't see them anymore) and fold away on the dotted yellow lines (you'll still be able to see them along the outside of the creases).

1. Cut the dragon Rings apart as shown.

2. Take one Ring and fold along line 1.

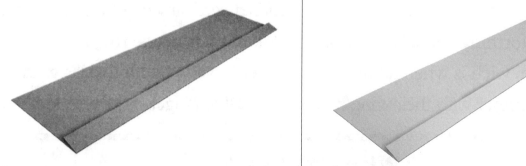

3. Fold along line 2.

4. Fold along line 3.

5. Fold along line 4.

6. Roll the plane into a tube with the folds on the inside. Slip one edge of the fold into the other, so they interlock. Tape the tube closed.

Blue Angels and Thunderbirds

he Blue Angels and the Thunderbirds are the aerobatic flying teams for the U.S. Navy and Air Force, respectively. Each team consists of eight jet fighters that travel around the country performing stunts and flying in formation, wich is when all the planes fly together with their wing tips only inches apart. These performances demonstrate the amazing maneuverability of jet fighters and the skill of their pilots. You, too, can practice your piloting skills with your own Blue Angels and Thunderbirds.

WHAT TO DO IF...

YOUR PLANE DIVES AND CRASHES: Add up elevator by bending the back edges of the wings up a little. Or throw the plane a little harder.

YOUR PLANE CLIMBS, SLOWS, THEN CRASHES: Reduce the amount of up elevator by making the back edges of the tails flatter. Or throw the plane a little slower.

YOUR PLANE HEADS OFF TO THE RIGHT: Bend the rudder a little to the left.

YOUR PLANE HEADS OFF TO THE LEFT: Bend the rudder a little to the right.

NOTE: Small paper airplanes are more sensitive to adjustments, so make sure all your adjustments are small ones.

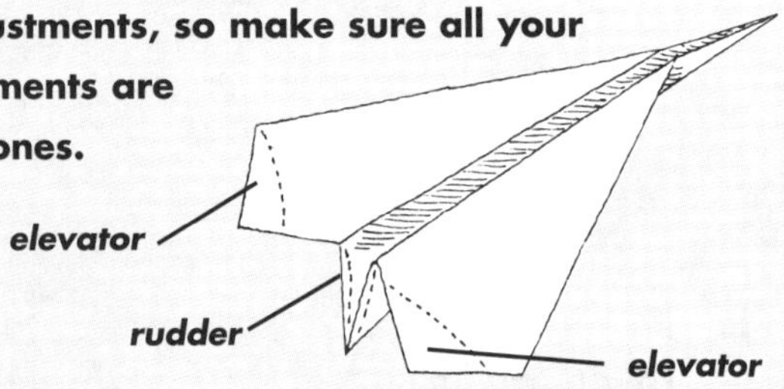

elevator

rudder

elevator

Making the Blue Angels and Thunderbirds

Don't forget: Cut along the solid white lines. Fold in on the dashed yellow lines (so you can't see them anymore) and fold away on the dotted red lines (you'll still be able to see them along the outside of the creases). **Folding tip:** Because these planes are so small, their folds can get bulky. Make your creases as sharp as possible.

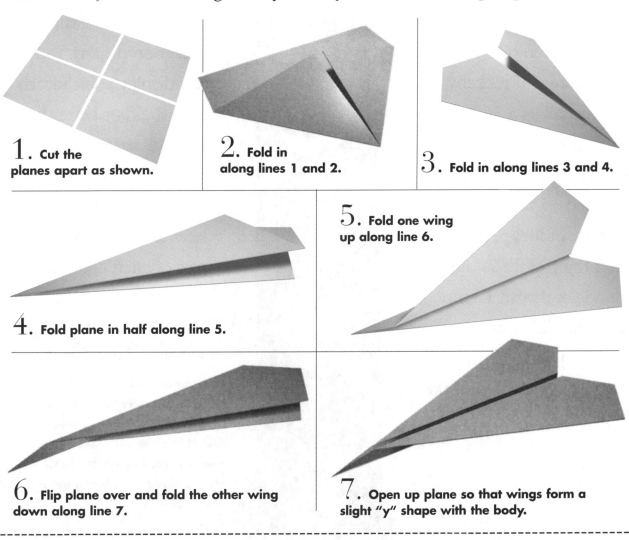

1. **Cut the planes apart as shown.**

2. **Fold in along lines 1 and 2.**

3. **Fold in along lines 3 and 4.**

4. **Fold plane in half along line 5.**

5. **Fold one wing up along line 6.**

6. **Flip plane over and fold the other wing down along line 7.**

7. **Open up plane so that wings form a slight "y" shape with the body.**

Saturn Rocket

 Your Saturn Rocket was impired by the real Saturn V rocket, the rocket that first took man to the moon in July 1969. There were 13 Saturn Vs launched between 1967 and 1973; six of them put men on the moon.

The Saturn V rocket was huge–as tall as a 35-story building–and at takeoff it weighed 6 million pounds.

It used 15 tons (30,000 pounds) of fuel per second at liftoff to produce $7\frac{1}{2}$ million pounds of thrust. Twenty thousand different companies produced parts for the rocket, and 500,000 people worked on it.

Your rocket isn't quiet that big or complicated, and doesn't produce all that smoke or noise either.

If you're in Cape Canaveral, Florida, you can see a real Saturn V rocket on display. You can display your Saturn on a shelf, or better yet, set up a spaceport in your bedroom. Then you can launch a mission to the kitchen nad recover samples of alien cookies.

WHAT TO DO IF...

This paper rocket was designed to be flown with the imagination. You will notice, however, that if it's actually thrown, it doesn't want to go straight. This can be fixed by adding tape and paper

Making the Saturn Rocket

1. Cut out the rocket as shown.

2. Shape the nose into a cone. Holding the bottom edges of the wedge, overlap the pieces to the pink line and tape the cone closed. Don't worry if you have to squish the cone a little in taping it. You can smooth it into the right shape when you've finished.

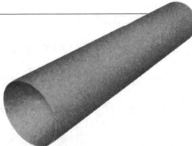

3. Roll the rocket body into a tube, overlapping the edges to the pink line, and tape the tube closed. If it makes it easier for you, use paper clips to hold the tube closed while you tape it. Make sure to put a peace of tape at the top, middle, and bottom of the tube.

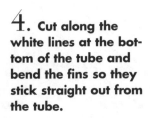

4. Cut along the white lines at the bottom of the tube and bend the fins so they stick straight out from the tube.

5. Place the nose cone on top of the tube and tape it in place. Use at least two pieces of tape, on opposite sides from each other. Prepare for lunch.

THE World Record Paper Airplane

This model is the king of the hill. It has held the Guinness World Record for time aloft since 1983. I came up with the design when I was 13 years old, and haven't come across a better paper glider since. Its longest officially recorded flight took place on February 17, 1994, and lasted 18.8 seconds. Try throwing it high into the air outdoors for spectacular flights.

WHAT TO DO IF...

YOUR PLANE DIVES AND CRASHES: Add up elevator by bending the back edges of the wings up a little. Or throw the plane a little harder.

YOUR PLANE CLIMBS, SLOWS, THEN CRASHES: Reduce the amount of up elevator by making the back edges of the tails flatter. Or throw the plane a little slower.

YOUR PLANE HEADS OFF TO THE RIGHT: Bend the rudder a little to the left.

YOUR PLANE HEADS OFF TO THE LEFT: Bend the rudder a little to the right.

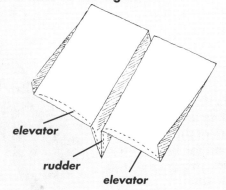

elevator

rudder

elevator

Making the World Record Paper Airplane

Don't forget: Fold in on the dashed blue lines (so you can't see them anymore) and fold away on the dotted red lines (you'll still be able to see them along the outside of the creases). **Folding Tip:** This model can get a little bulky in the nose, so make your creases as sharp as possible. You may also find that the paper from folds 1 and 2 bunches up as you make folds 3 through 10. Make a crease and flatten it down as you go along.

1. Fold in along lines 1 and 2.

2. Fold up along line 3 to line 4.

3. Continue folding up along lines 4 through 9.

4. Fold along line 10.

5. Flip plane over and fold in half along line 11.

6. Fold one wing down along line 12.

7. Flip plane over and fold the other wing down along line 13.

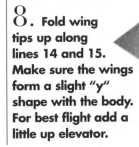

8. Fold wing tips up along lines 14 and 15. Make sure the wings form a slight "y" shape with the body. For best flight add a little up elevator.

Flying Saucer

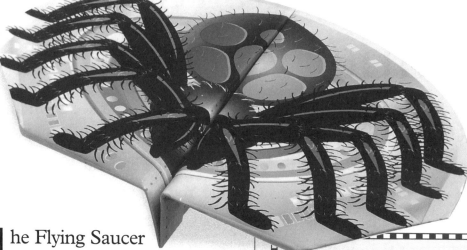

The Flying Saucer looks like a plane that could only have come from Mars. But, in fact, serveral round-winged airplanes have been made. In the 1930s, research scientist Charles Zimmerman designed a flying saucer airplane called the V-173 that flew well, but was never put into production. In the 1950s, a jet-powered saucer called the Avro Car was built. It took off and landed like a helicopter, but wasn't able to climb to flying altitudes, so no more were ever made. Still these efforts proved that flying saucers could fly.

WHAT TO DO IF...

YOUR PLANE DIVES AND CRASHES: Add up elevator by bending the back edges of the tails up a little. Or throw the plane a little harder.

YOUR PLANE CLIMBS, SLOWS, THEN CRASHES: Reduce the amount of up elevator by making the back edges of the tails flatter. Or throw the plane a little slower.

YOUR PLANE HEADS OFF TO THE RIGHT: Bend the rudder a little to the left.

YOUR PLANE HEADS OFF TO THE LEFT: Bend the rudder a little to the right.

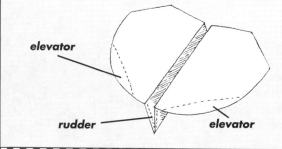

Making the Flying Saucer

Don't forget: Cut along the solid white lines. Fold in on the dashed pink lines (so you can't see them anymore) and fold away on the dotted yellow lines (you'll still be able to see them along the outside of the creases).

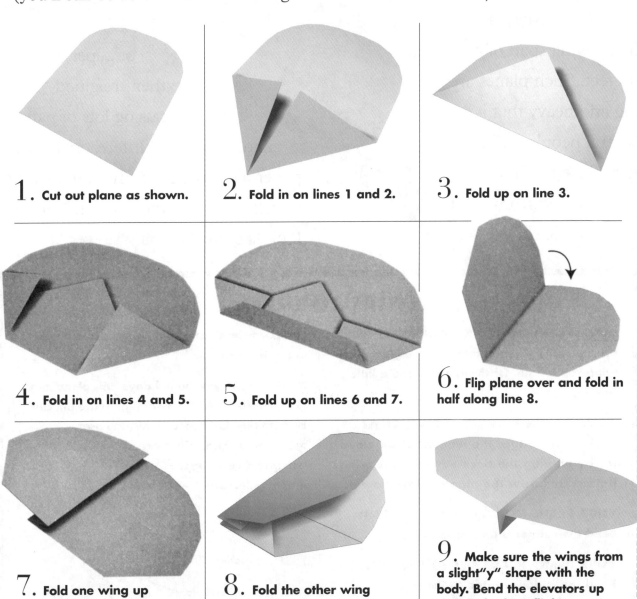

1. Cut out plane as shown.

2. Fold in on lines 1 and 2.

3. Fold up on line 3.

4. Fold in on lines 4 and 5.

5. Fold up on lines 6 and 7.

6. Flip plane over and fold in half along line 8.

7. Fold one wing up along line 9.

8. Fold the other wing down along line 10.

9. Make sure the wings from a slight "y" shape with the body. Bend the elevators up slightly for best flights.

THE Great White

This is a big paper airplane, though far from being the biggest. The world's largest paper airplane on record had a wing span of more than 45 feet. Such planes are so big and heavy that it takes several people to lift and throw them. They aren't folded from an extra big sheet of paper, but rather are glued together using lots of paper and cardboard. Interestingly, big paper airplanes fly at the same speed as regular-size paper planes, but they look like they're going slower.

WHAT TO DO IF...

YOUR PLANE DIVES AND CRASHES: Add up elevator by bending the back edges of the wings up a little. Or throw the plane a little harder.

YOUR PLANE CLIMBS, SLOWS, THEN CRASHES: Reduce the amount of up elevator by making the back edges of the wings flatter. Or throw the plane a little slower.

YOUR PLANE HEADS OFF TO THE RIGHT: Bend the rudder a little to the left.

YOUR PLANE HEADS OFF TO THE LEFT: Bend the rudder a little to the right.

For extra-steady straight flights, add a paper clip to the nose.

NOTE: On rainy or humid days, this plane may get a little limp. All paper airplanes are affected by humidity, but because this one uses more paper, it absorbs more water and gets floppier than regular-size planes.

elevator

rudder

elevator

Making the Great White

Note: This plane uses 2 sheets of paper. Side 1B overlaps Side 1A at the black line so that the green backgrounds match up. **Don't forget:** Cut along the solid white lines. Fold in on the dashed yellow lines (so you can't see them anymore) and fold away on the dotted red lines (you'll still be able to see them along the outside of the creases).

1. Tape together the two sheets of the Great White along the black line. Tape all the way across on both sides.

2. Fold in along lines 1 and 2.

3. Fold in along lines 3 and 4.

4. Flip plane over and fold in half along line 5. Cut along the solid line near the back of the fuselage.

5. Fold one wing down along line 6.

6. Flip plane over and fold the other wing down along line 7.

7. Open up the wings.

8. Push up tail and crease along lines 8 and 9.

9. Fold wing tips up along lines 10 and 11.

THE F-15

his plane was inspired by the McDonnell Douglas F-15 Eagle, one of the world's best jet fighters and the primary fighter of the U.S. Air Force since 1972. It has two huge engines that produce 50,000 pounds of thrust, allowing the plane to accelerate straight up, like a rocket. Some F-15s can climb from the ground to an altitude of seven miles in less than one minute. The engines also help the F-15 fly fast—up to two-and-one-half times the speed of sound (about 1,600 miles per hour). Your F-15 doesn't need jet engines; an easy toss will send it speeding across the room.

WHAT TO DO IF...

YOUR PLANE DIVES AND CRASHES: Add up elevator by bending the backs of the horizontal (flat) tails up a little.

YOUR PLANE CLIMBS, SLOWS, THEN CRASHES: Reduce the amount of up elevator by bending the backs of the horizontal (flat) tails down a little.
Or try adding weight to the nose (use bigger paper clip or add a few pieces of tape).

YOUR PLANE HEADS OFF TO THE RIGHT: Bend the back of the vertical tails (the ones that stick up) a little to the left.

YOUR PLANE HEADS OFF TO THE LEFT: Bend the back of the vertical tails (the ones that stick up) a little to the right.

NOTE: Inspect your plane after each landing and straighten any unwanted bends.

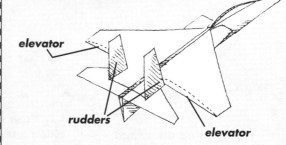

elevator

rudders

elevator

Making the F-15

Don't forget: Cut along the solid white lines. Fold in on the dashed yellow lines (so you can't see them anymore) and fold away on the dotted blue lines (you'll still be able to see them along the outside of the creases).

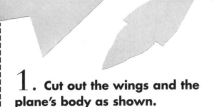

1. Cut out the wings and the plane's body as shown.

2. Fold the wings along lines 1 and 2, then put aside.

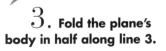

3. Fold the plane's body in half along line 3.

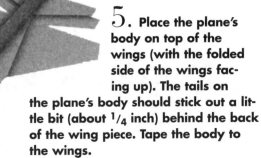

4. Fold down the engines along lines 4 and 6. Fold the trails down along lines 5 and 7.

5. Place the plane's body on top of the wings (with the folded side of the wings facing up). The tails on the plane's body should stick out a little bit (about ¼ inch) behind the back of the wing piece. Tape the body to the wings.

6. Flip the plane over and tape the front of the wing piece to the plane's body.

7. Fold up the top tails along lines 8 and 9. Slip a paper clip over the tip of the nose.

Flight Log

Pilots of real airplanes use their flight logs to record where they go, how long the flight takes, and interesting aspects of the trip. You can keep a similar log for your paper airplanes. You don't have to record every flight, but rather make entries for new planes, longest time aloft, greatest distances flown, and the like.

DATE	AIRPLANE NAME	WHERE	LONGEST TIME ALOFT	GREATEST DISTANCE FLOWN	NOTES

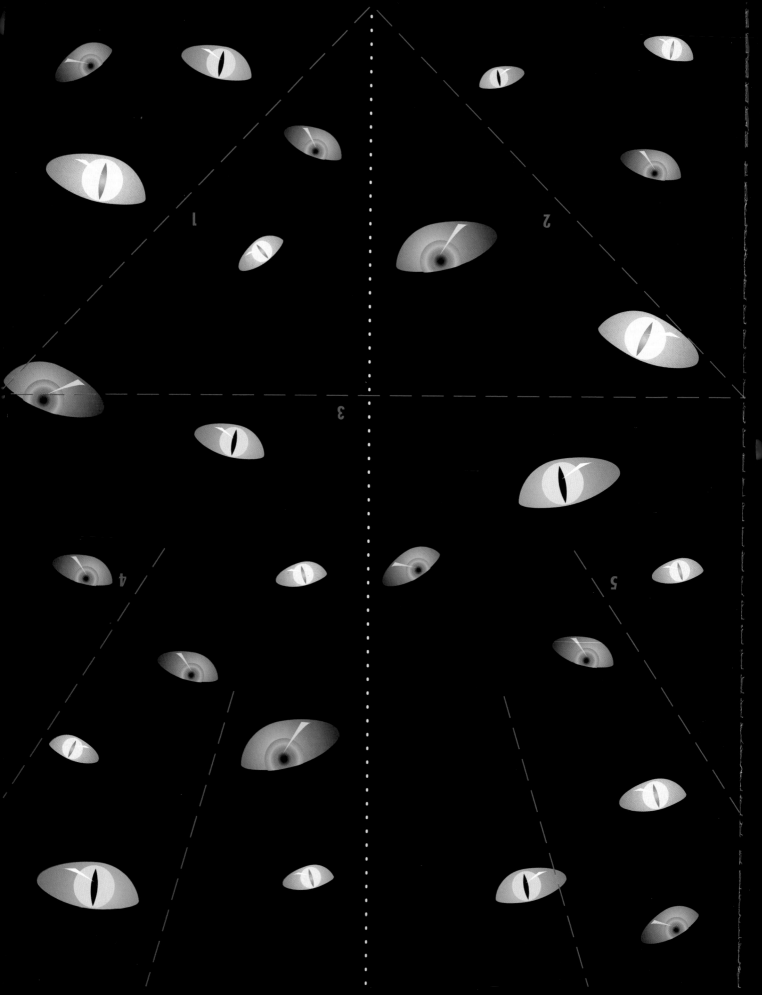

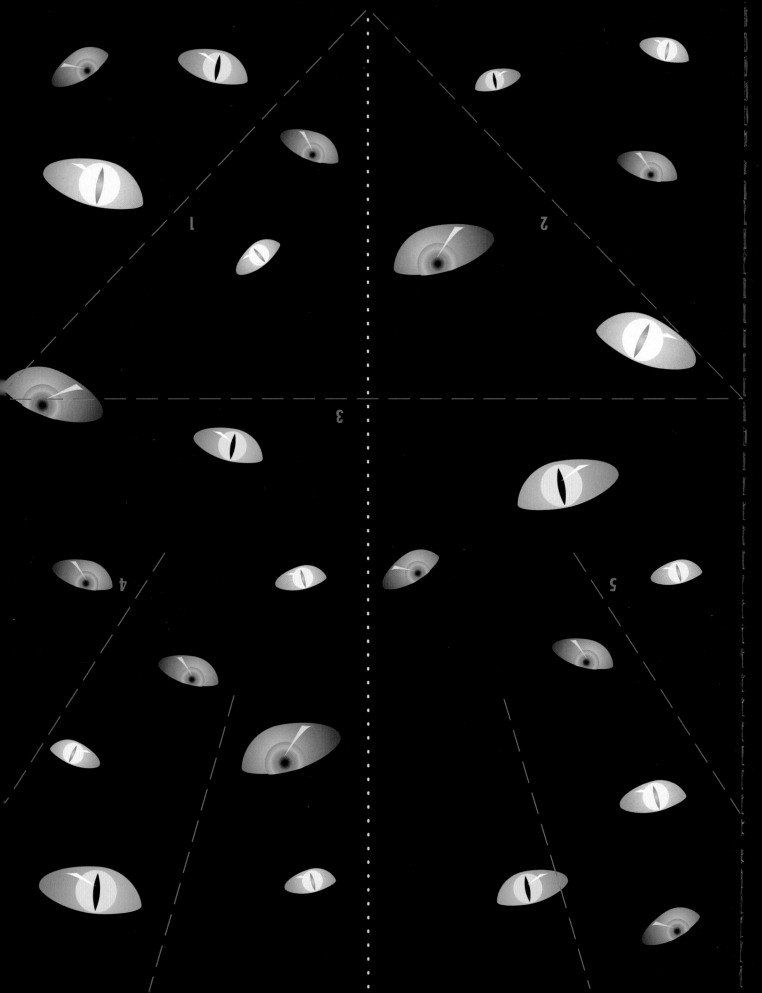

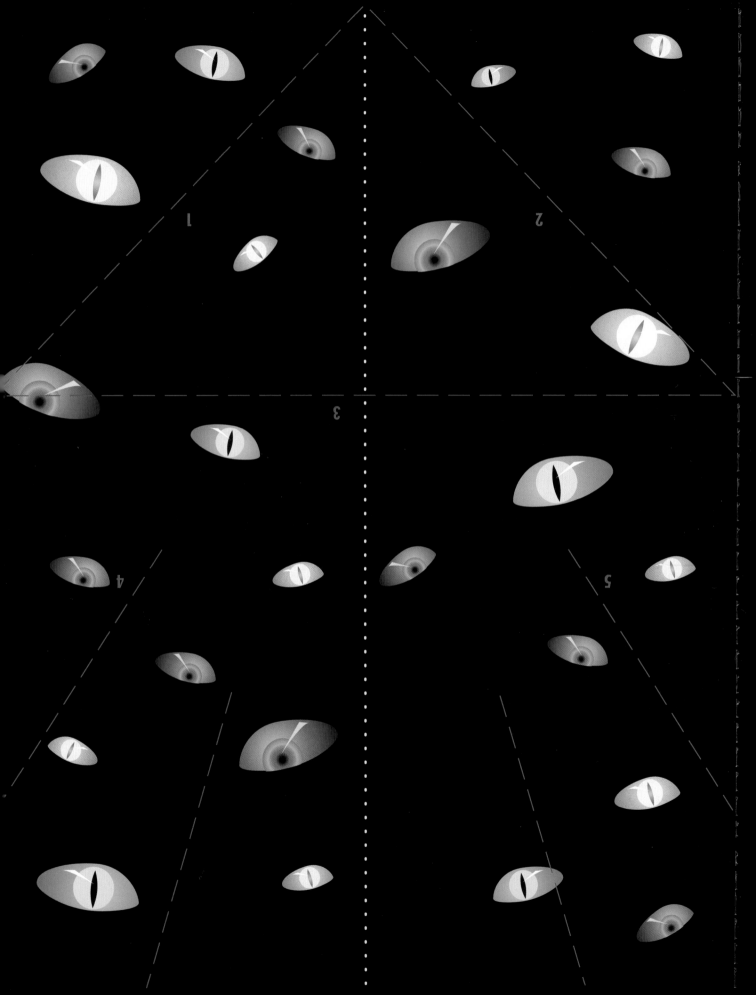

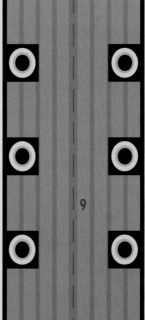

9

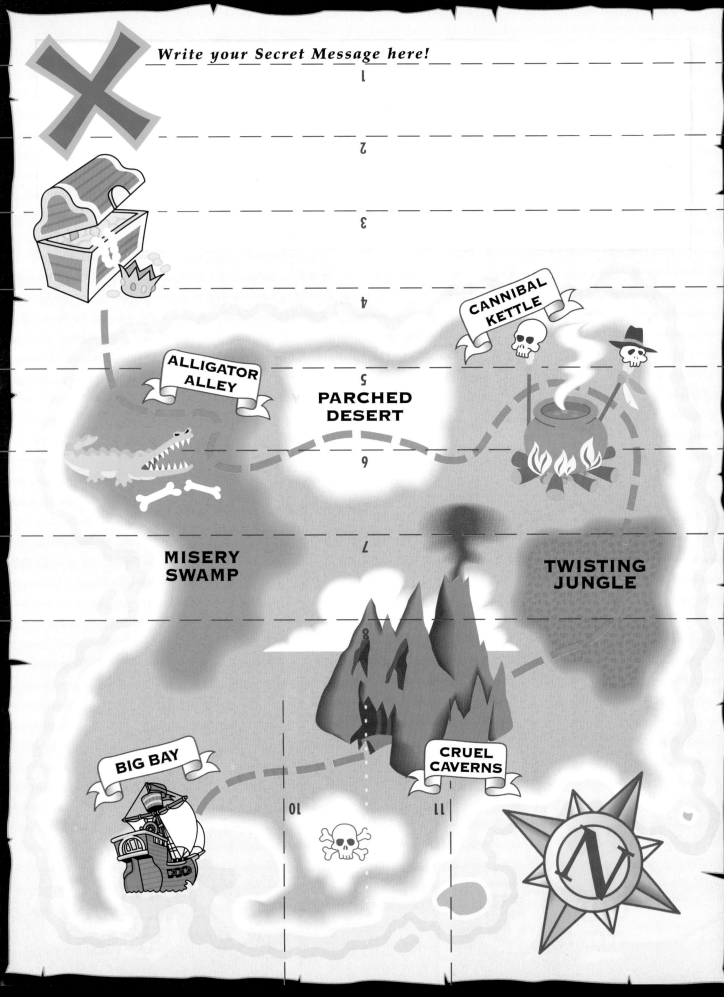

PIRATE'S SECRET

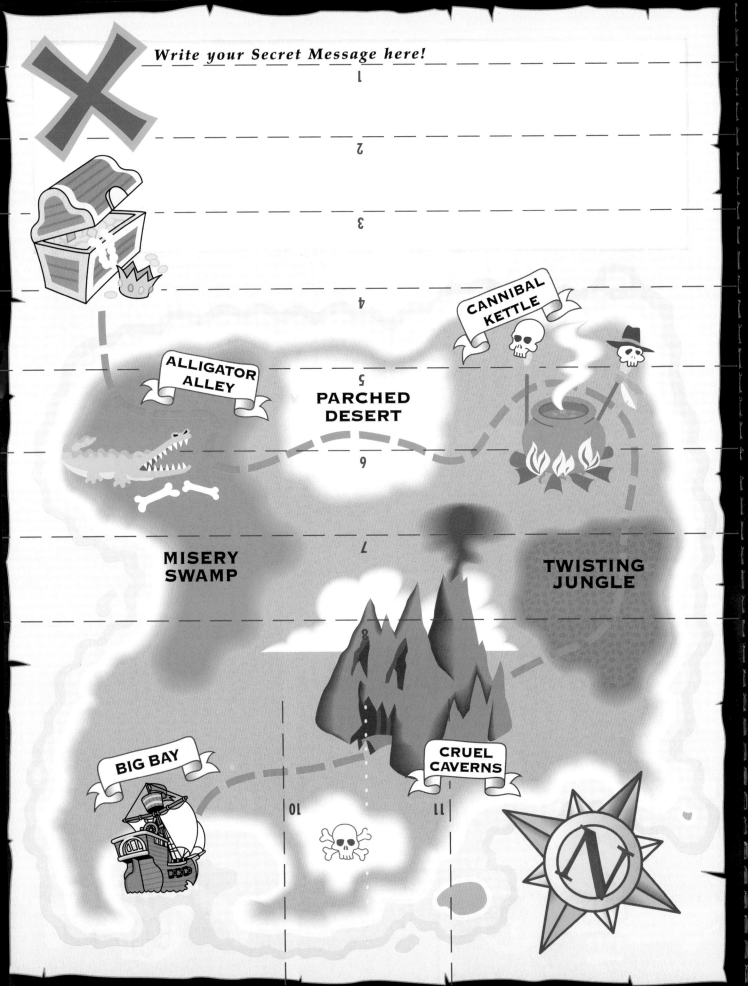

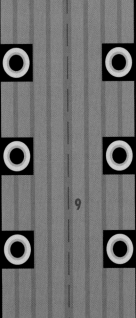

9

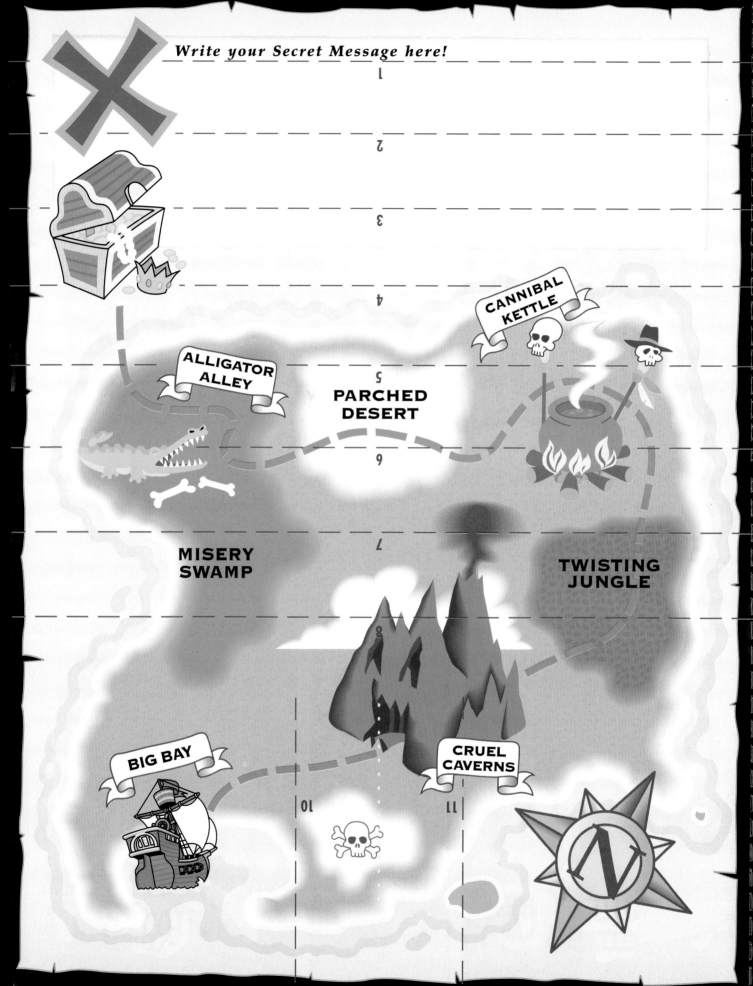

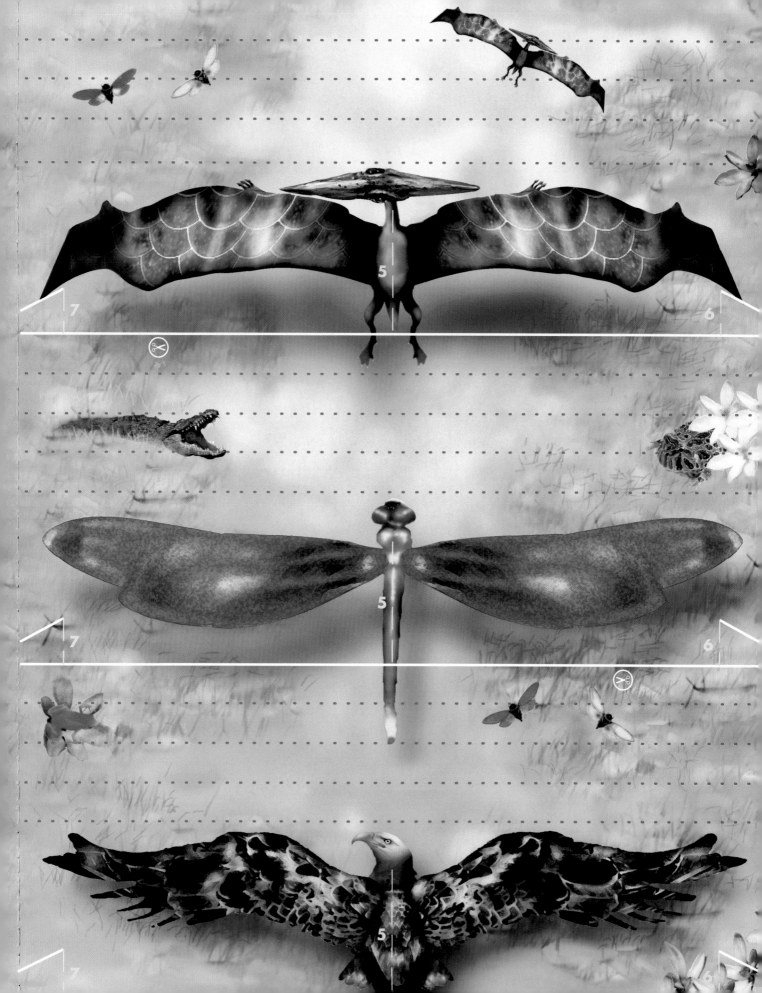

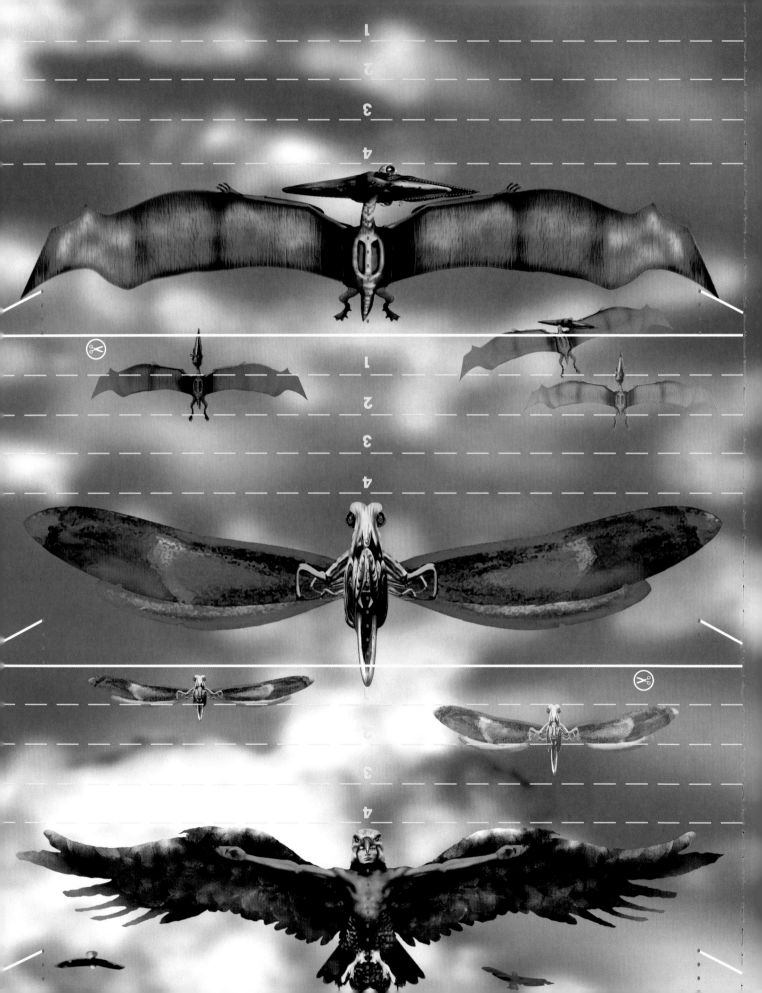

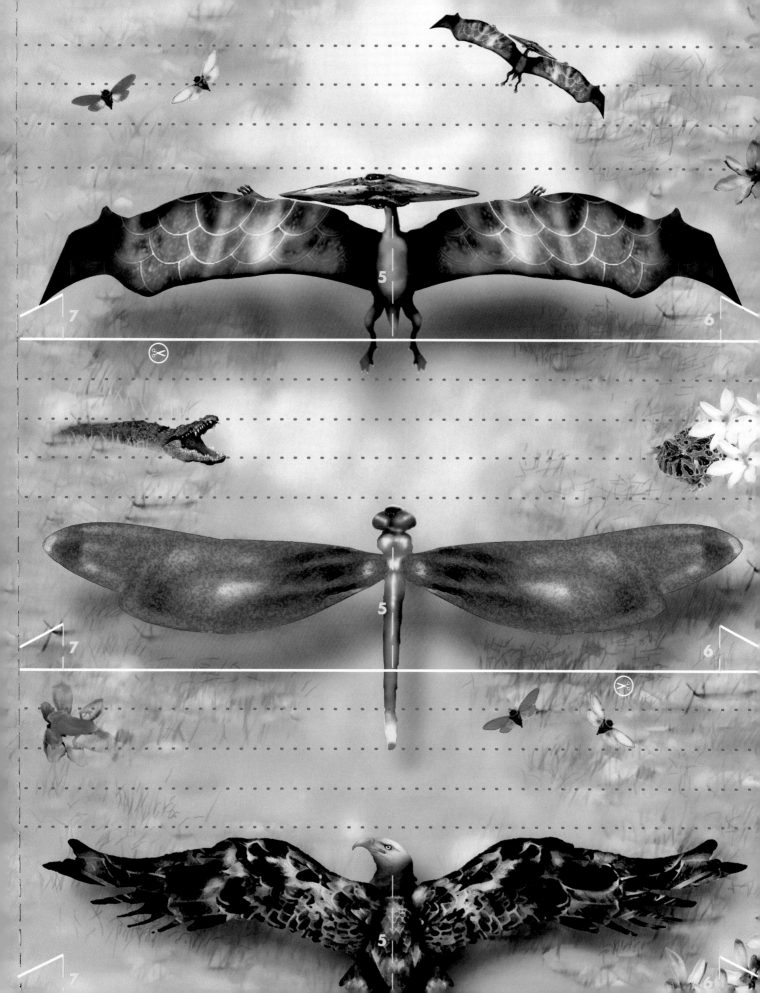

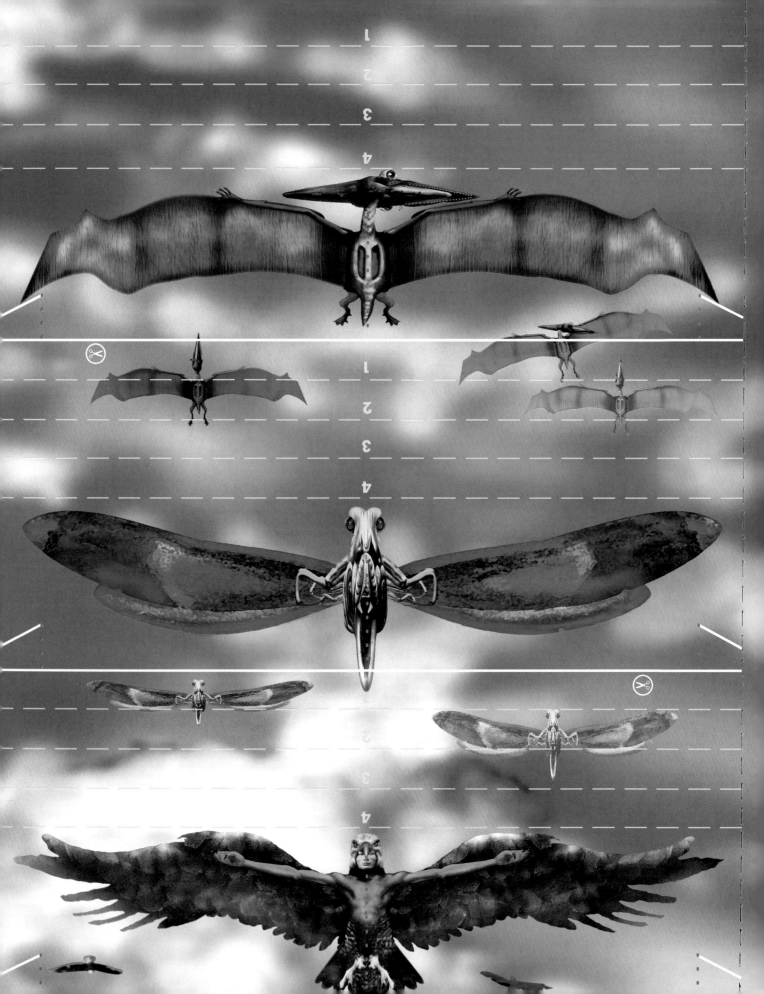

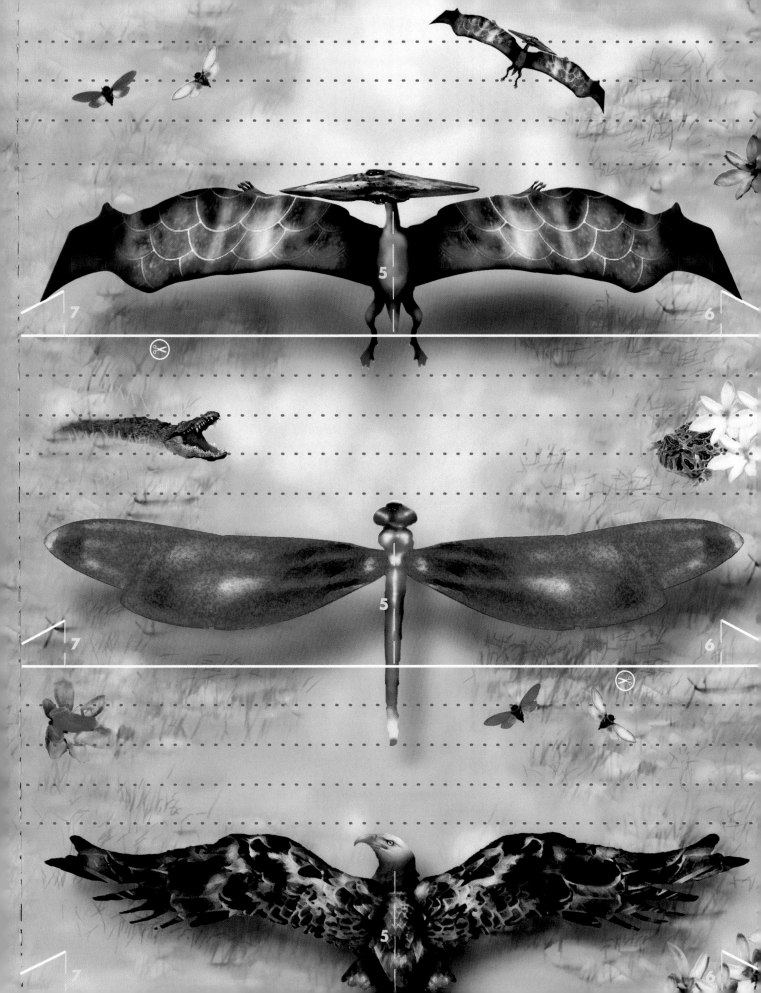

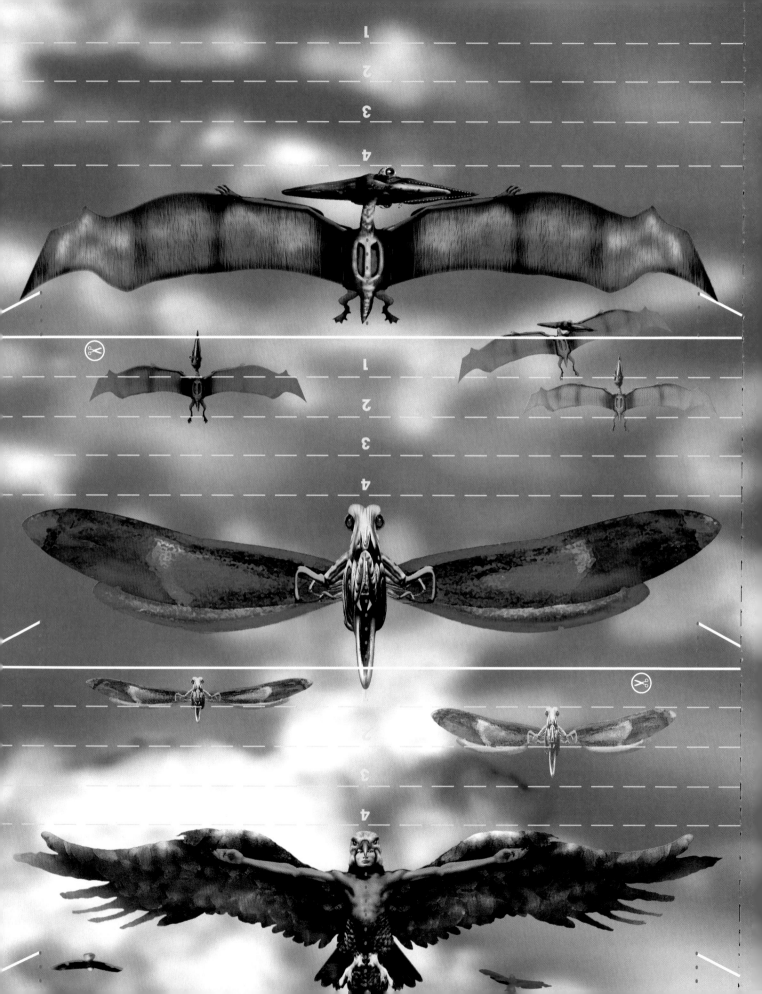

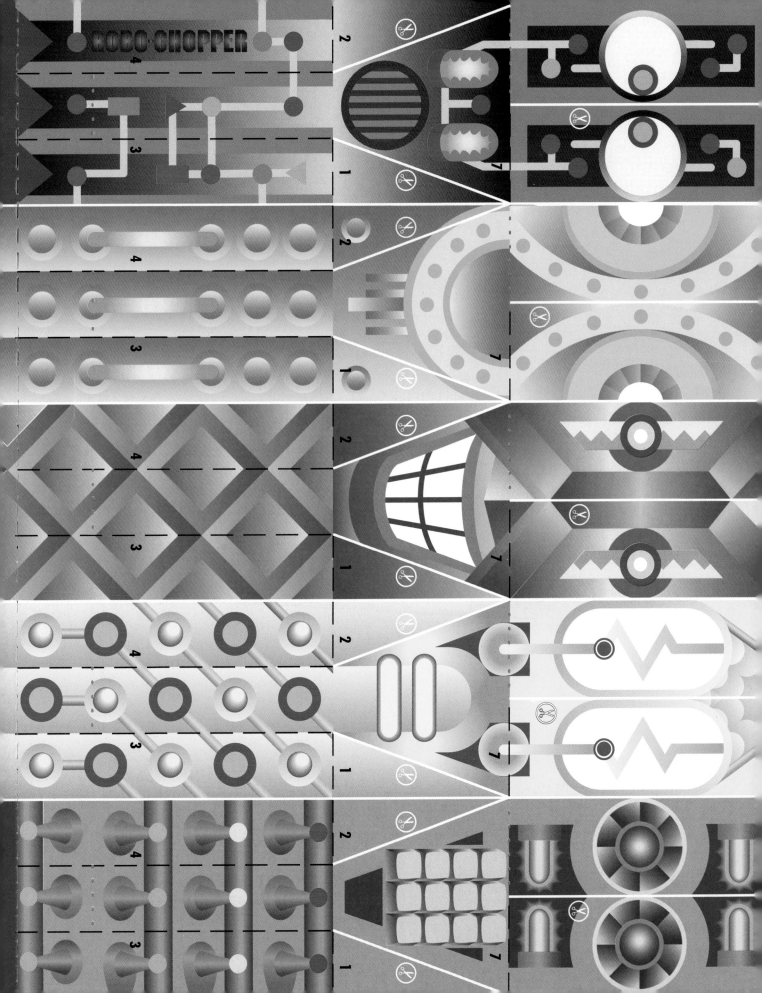

ROBO-CHOPPER

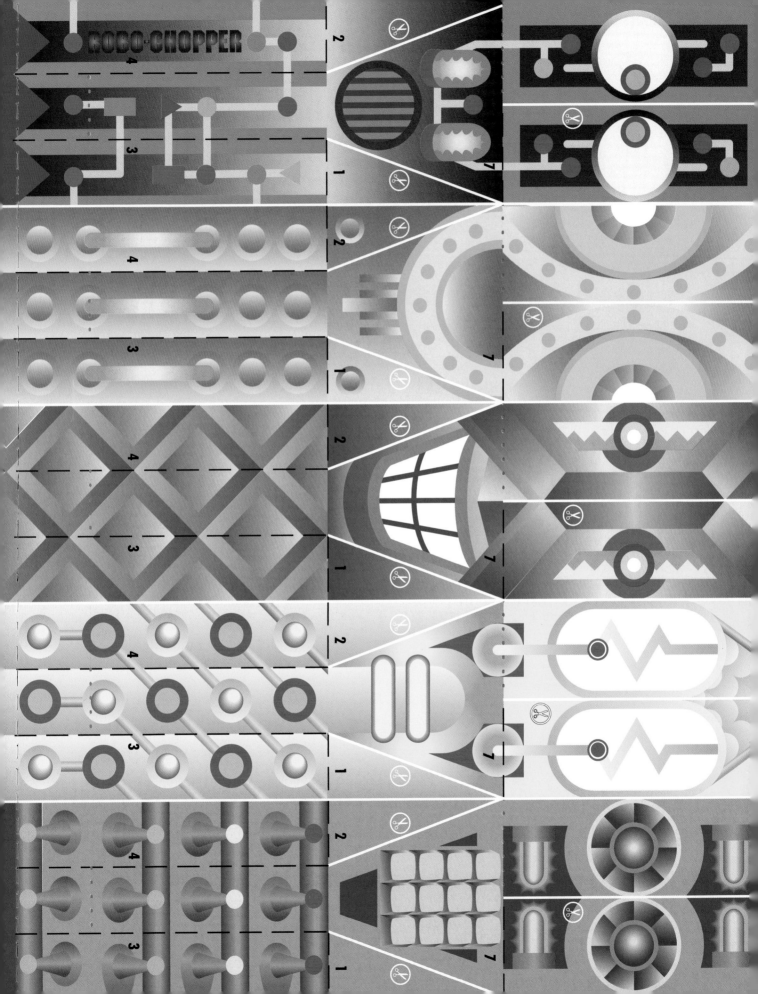

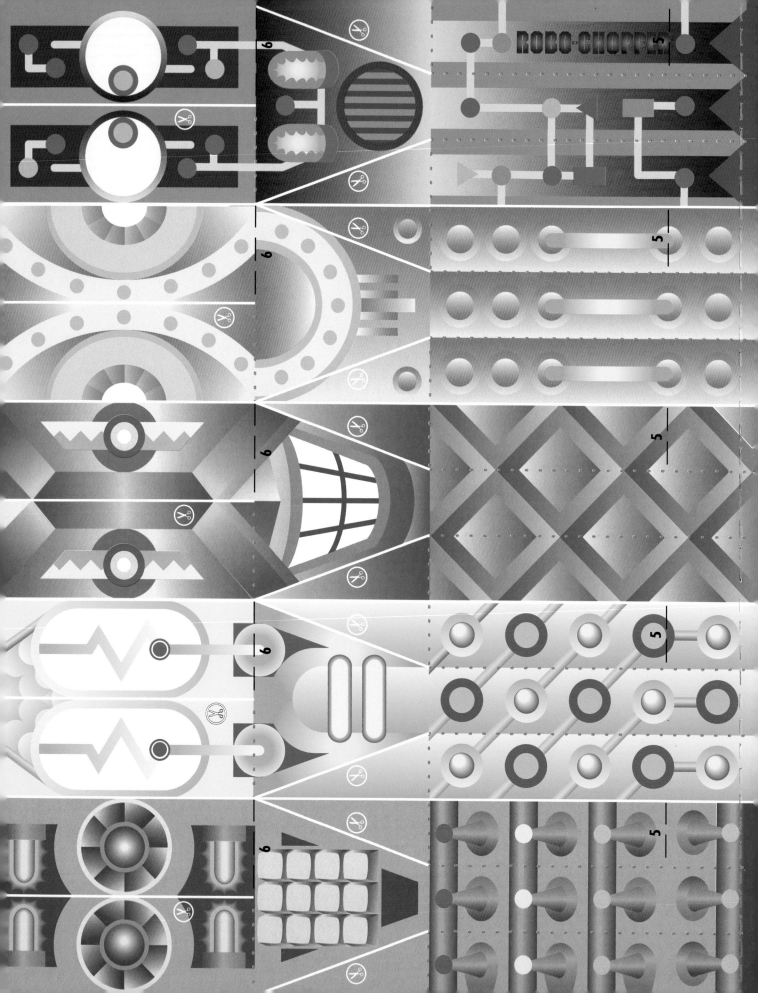

ROBO-CHOPPER

ROBO-CHOPPER

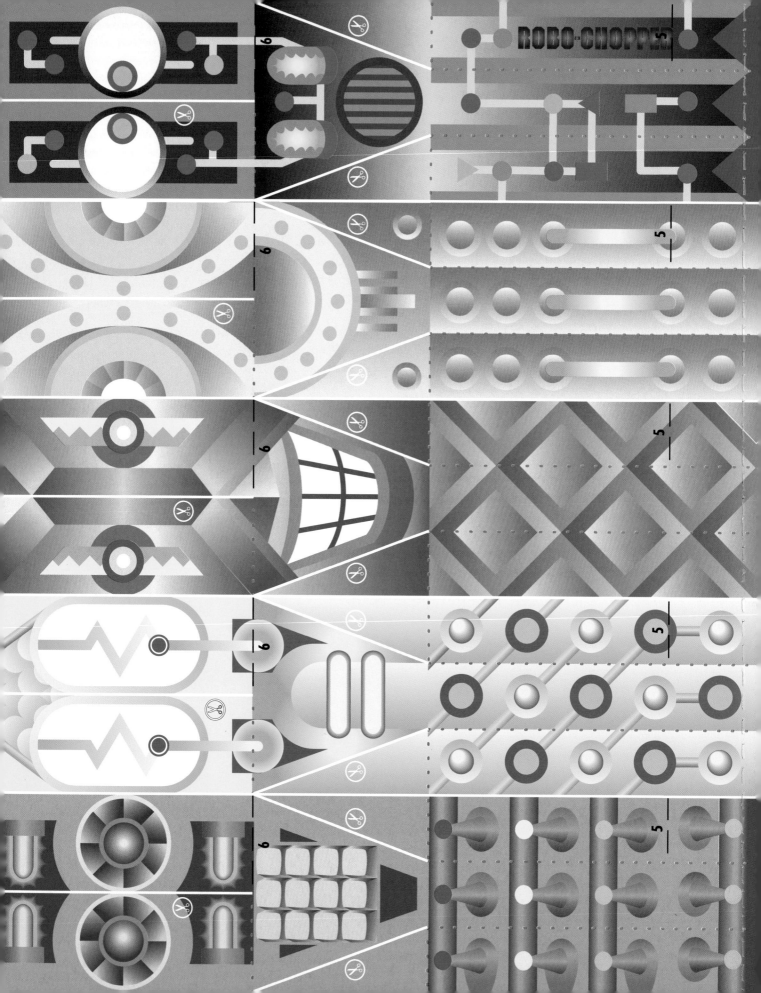

ROBO-CHOPPER

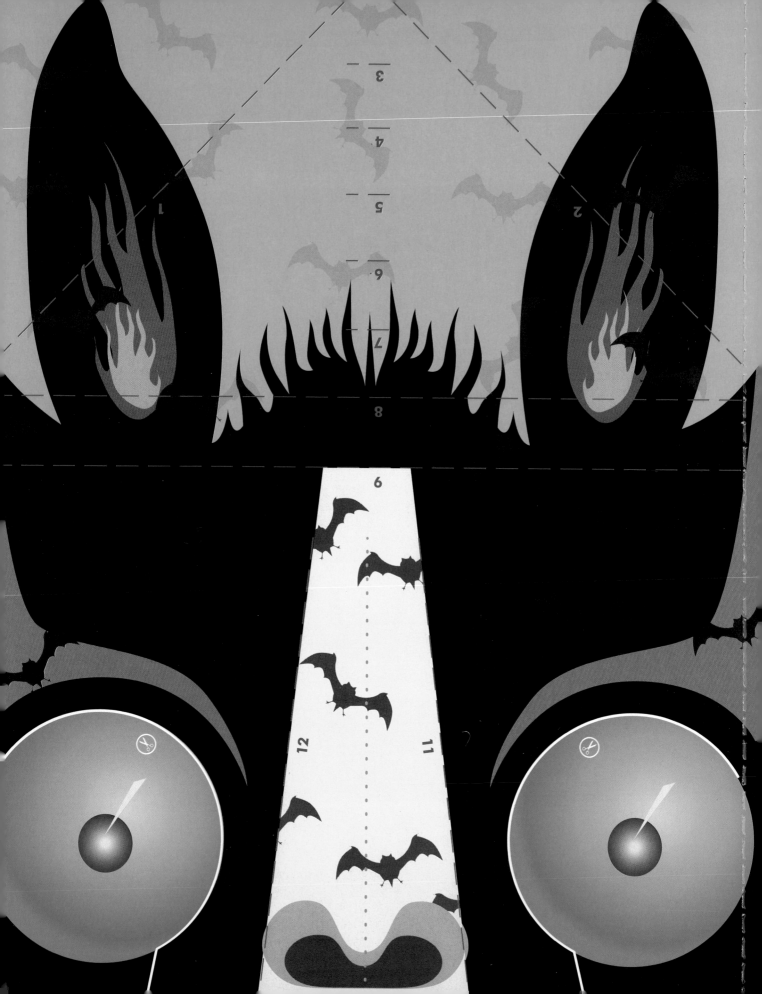

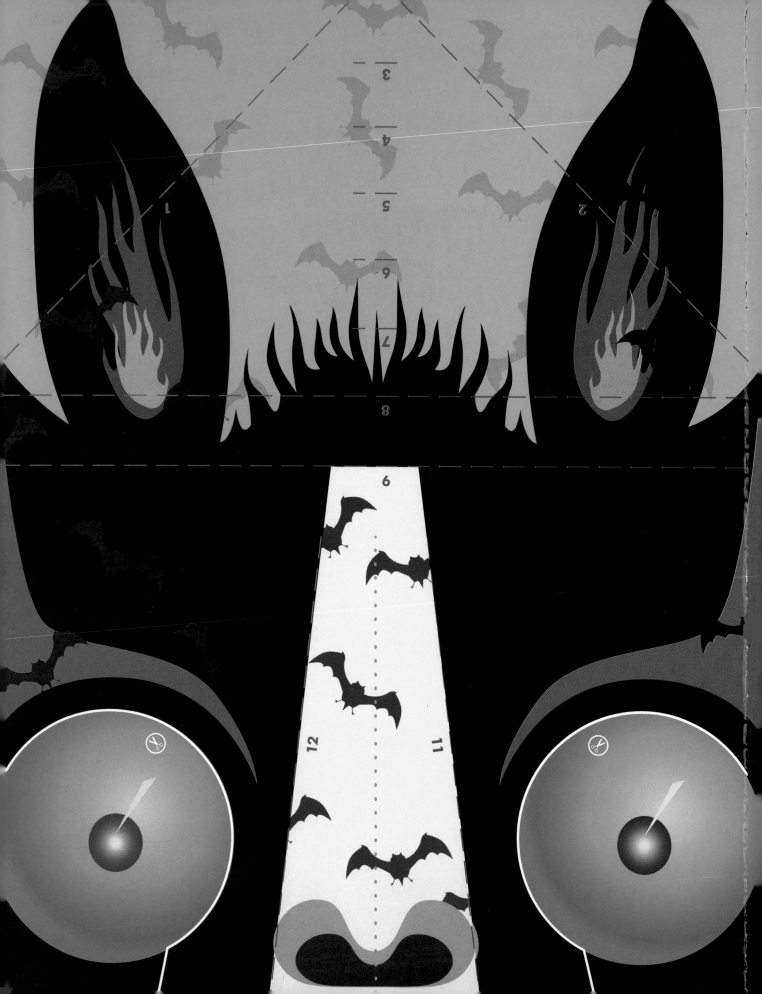

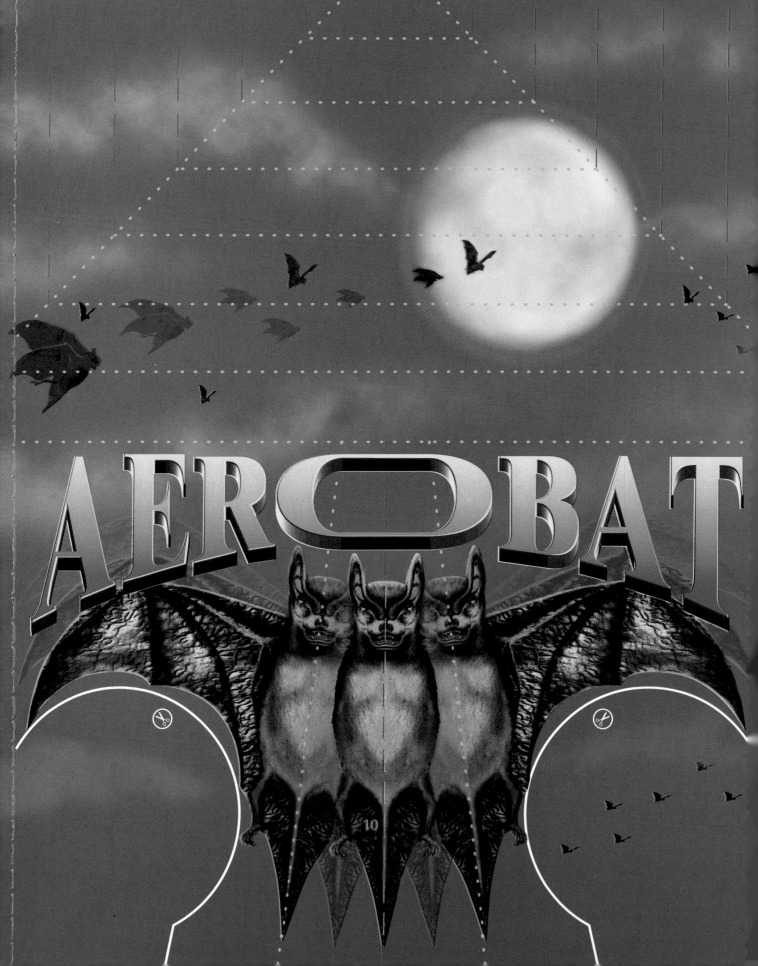

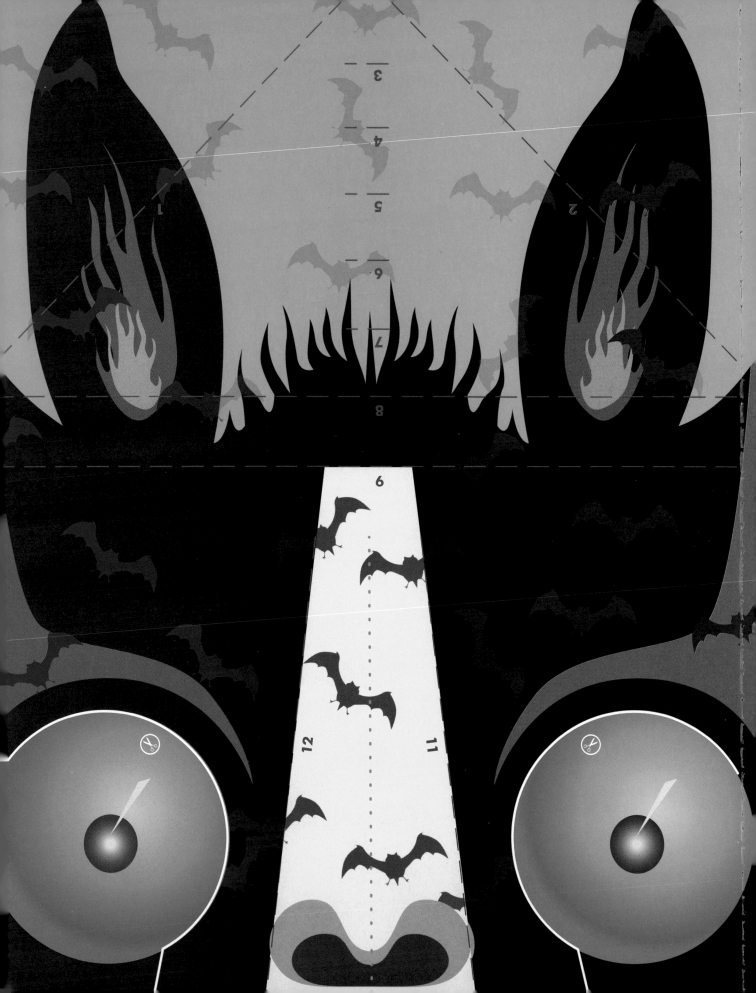

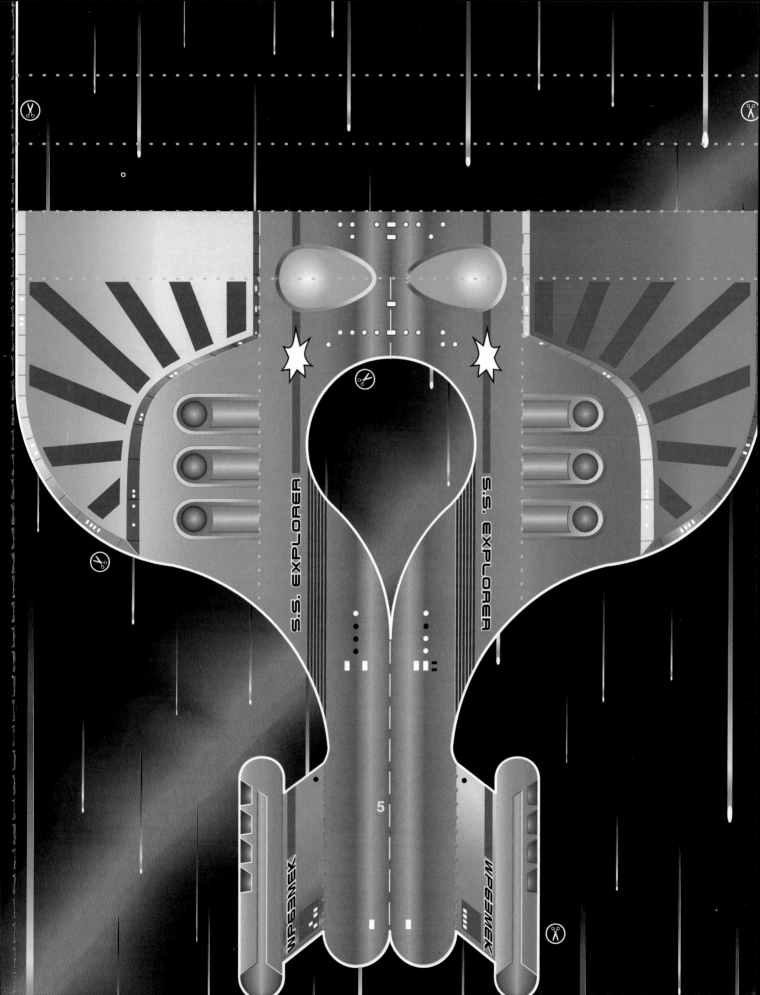

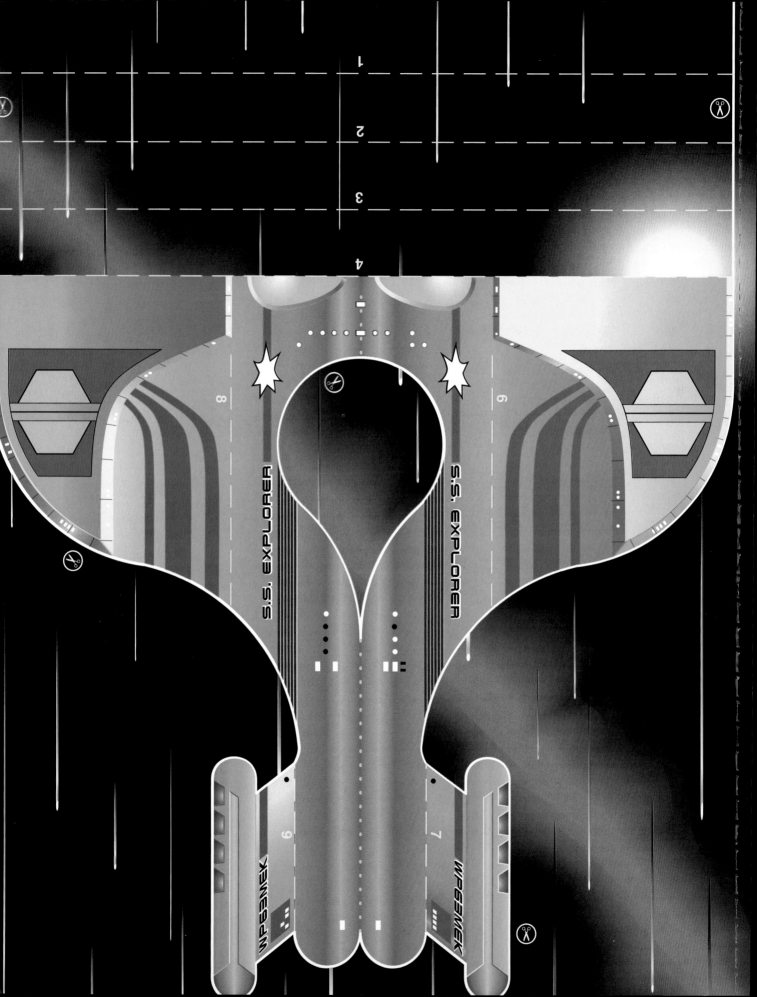

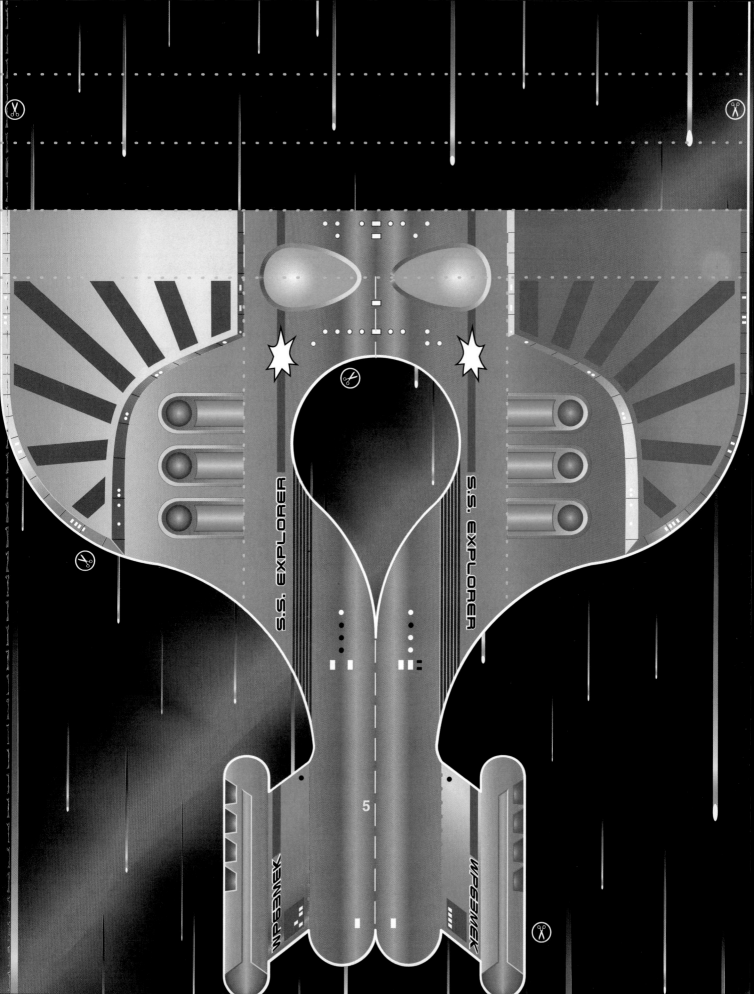

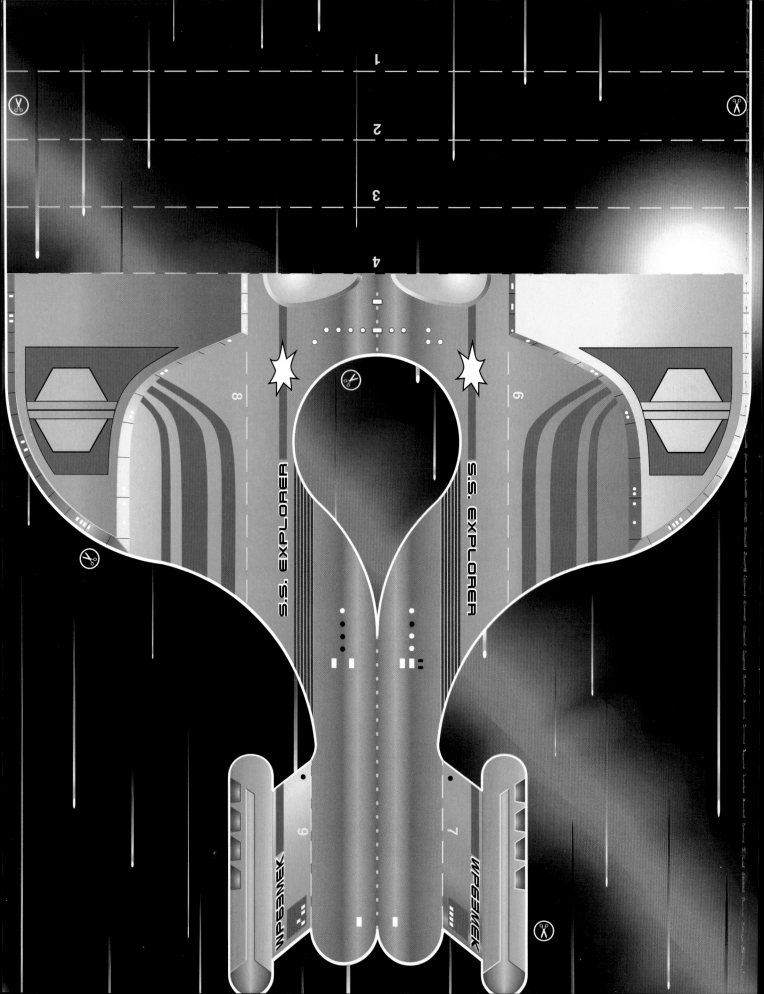

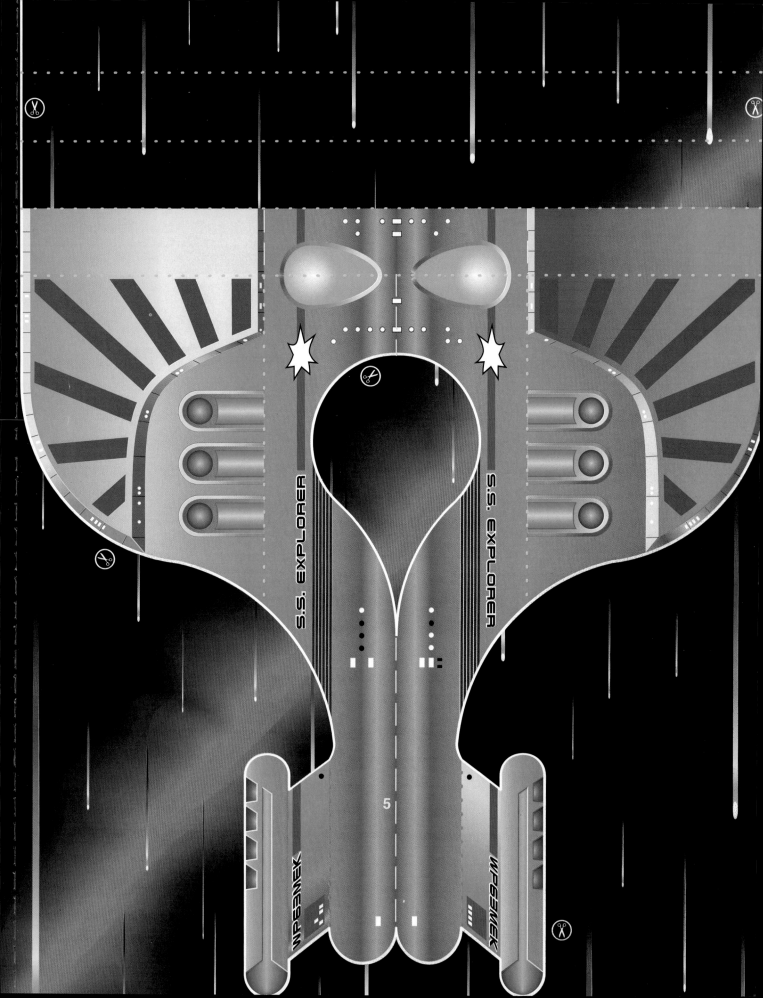

S.S. EXPLORER

5

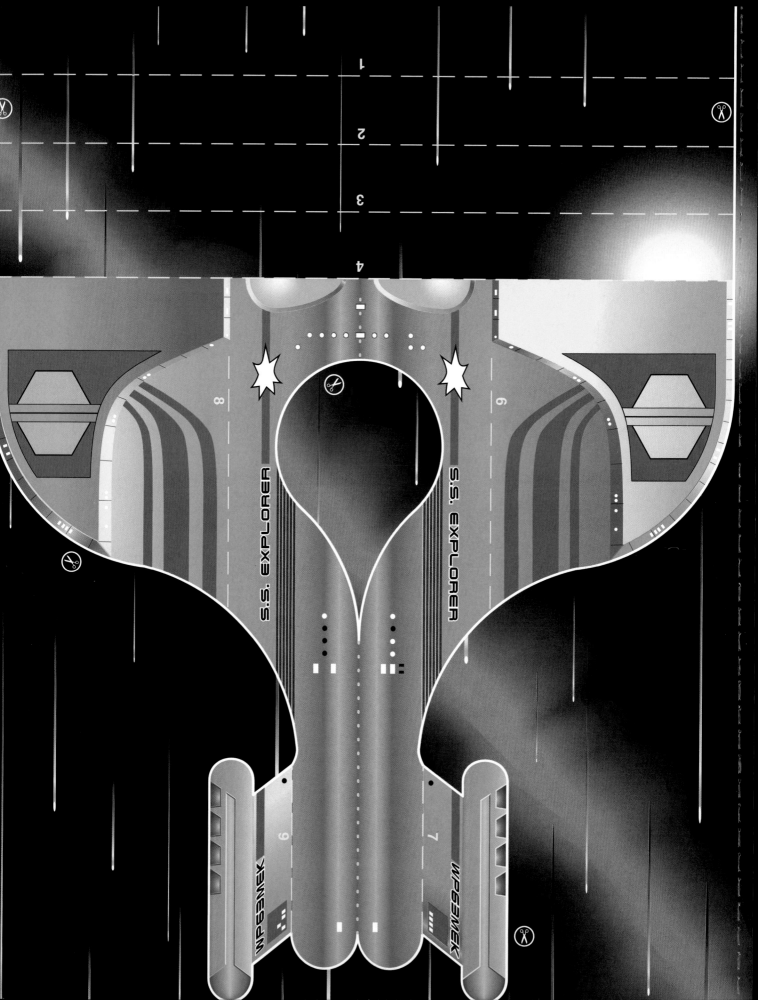

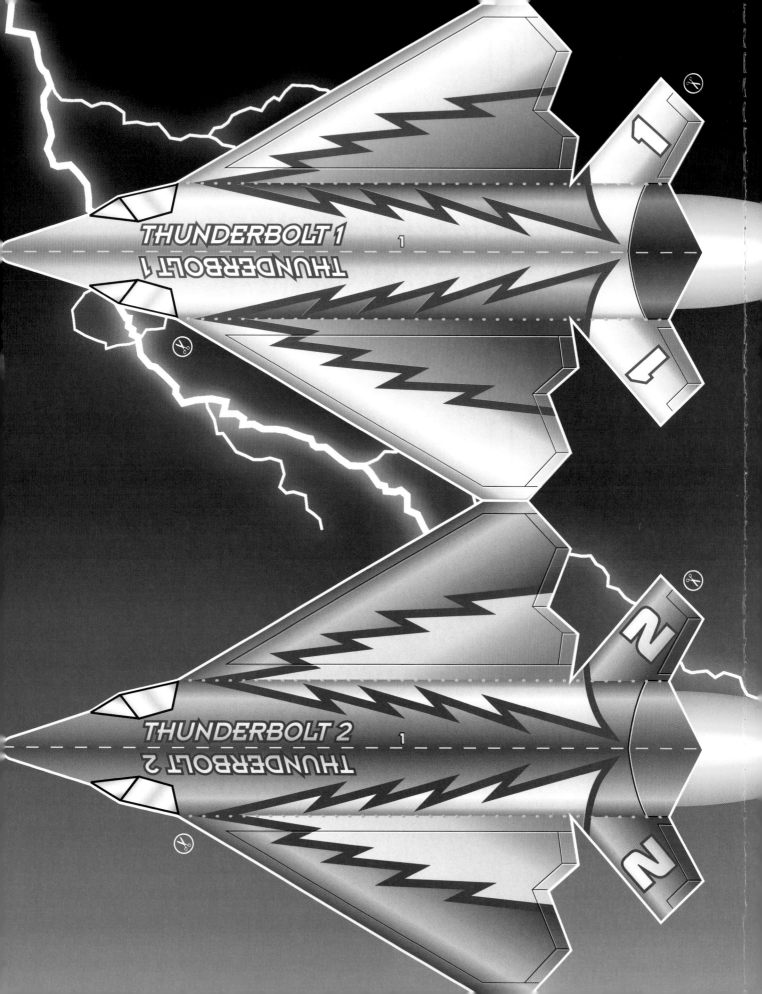

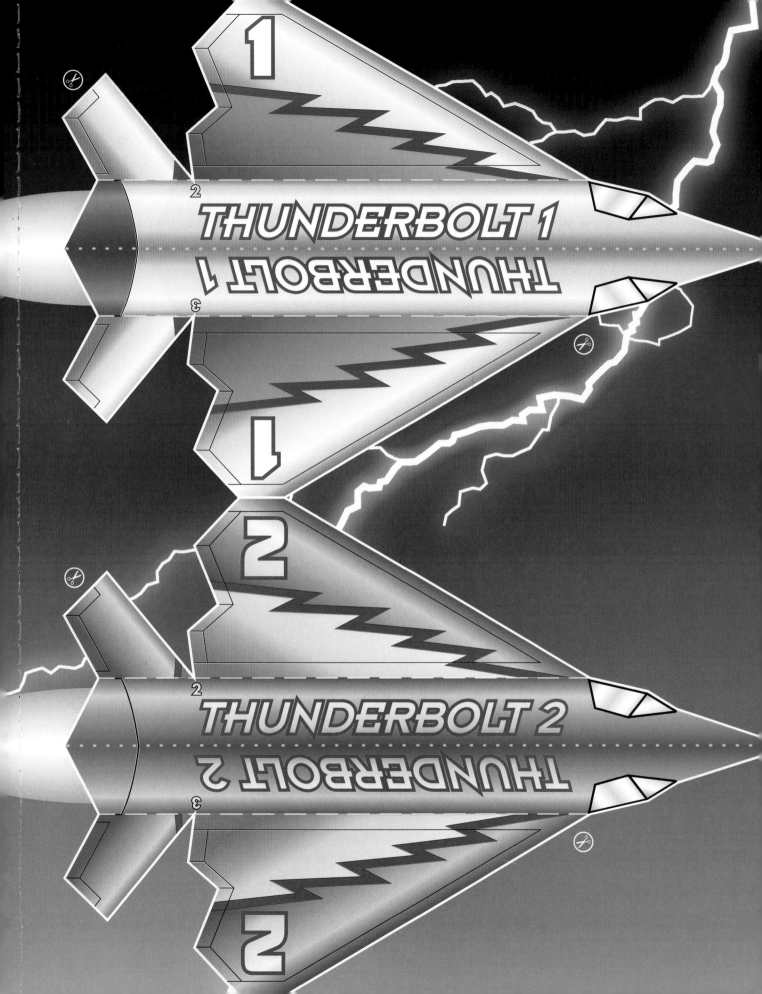

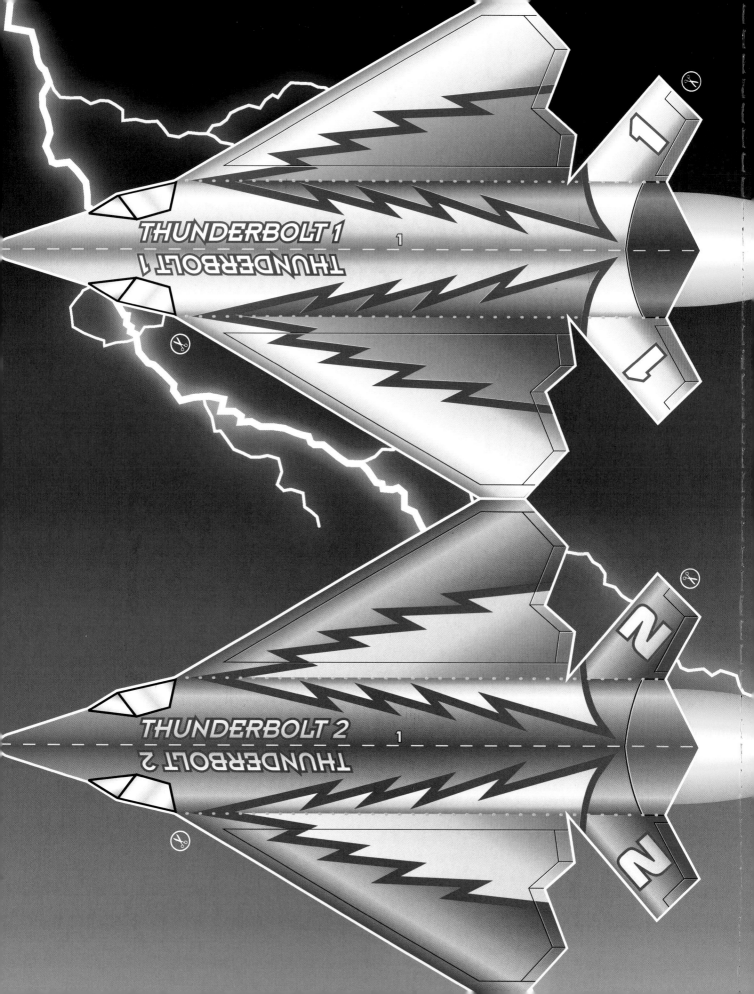

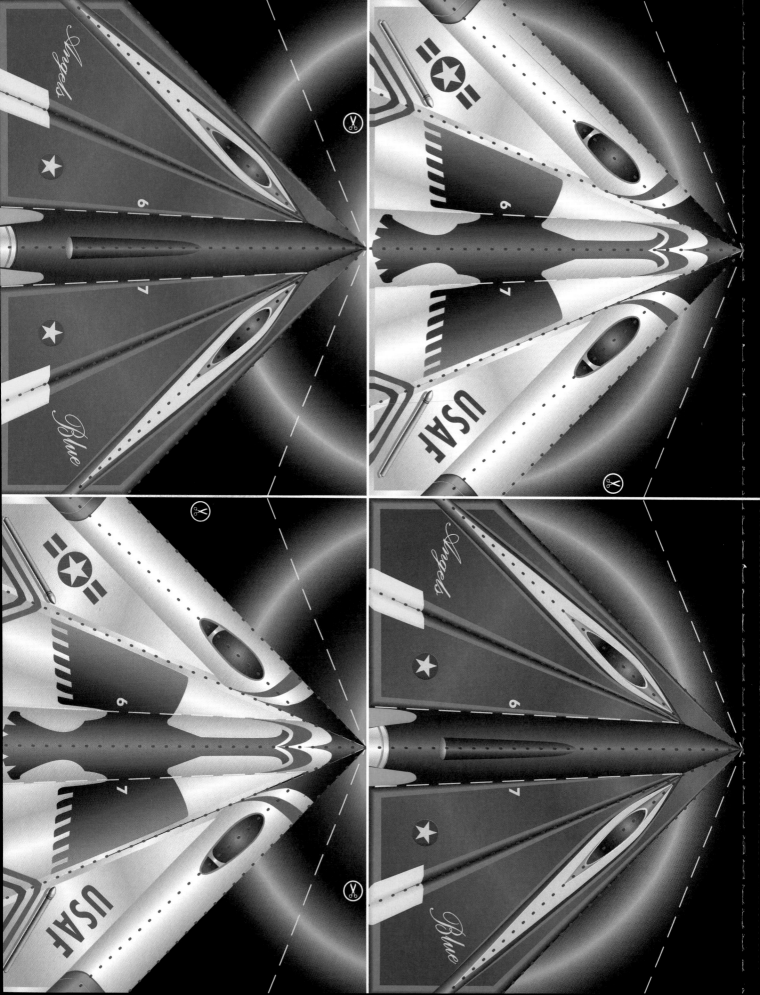

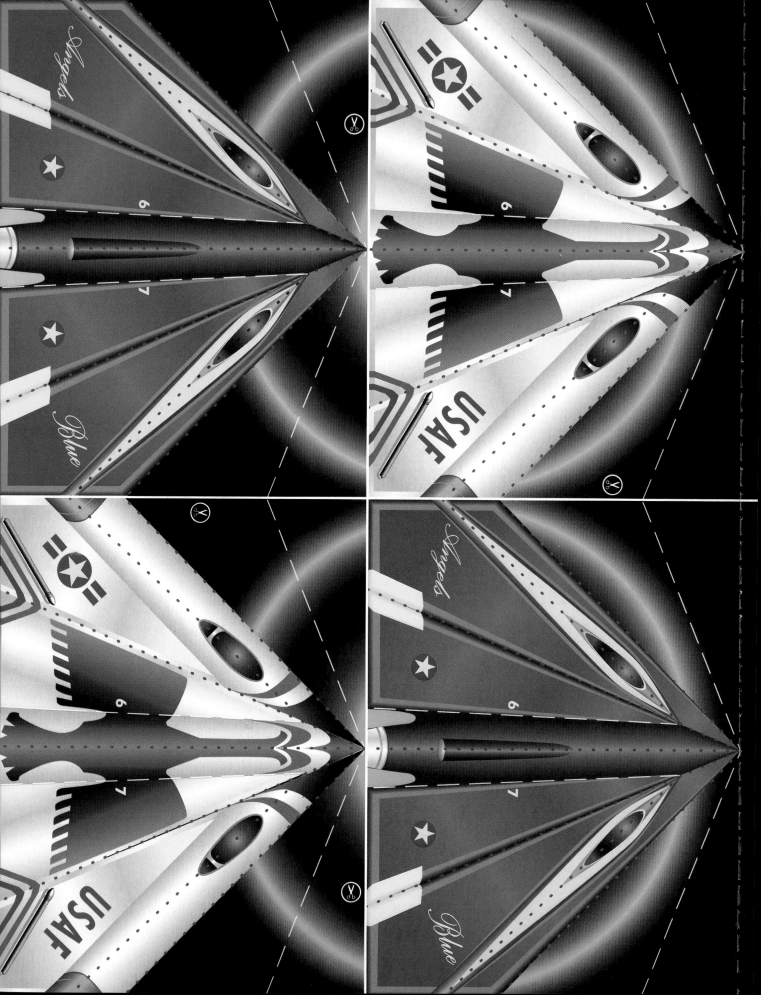

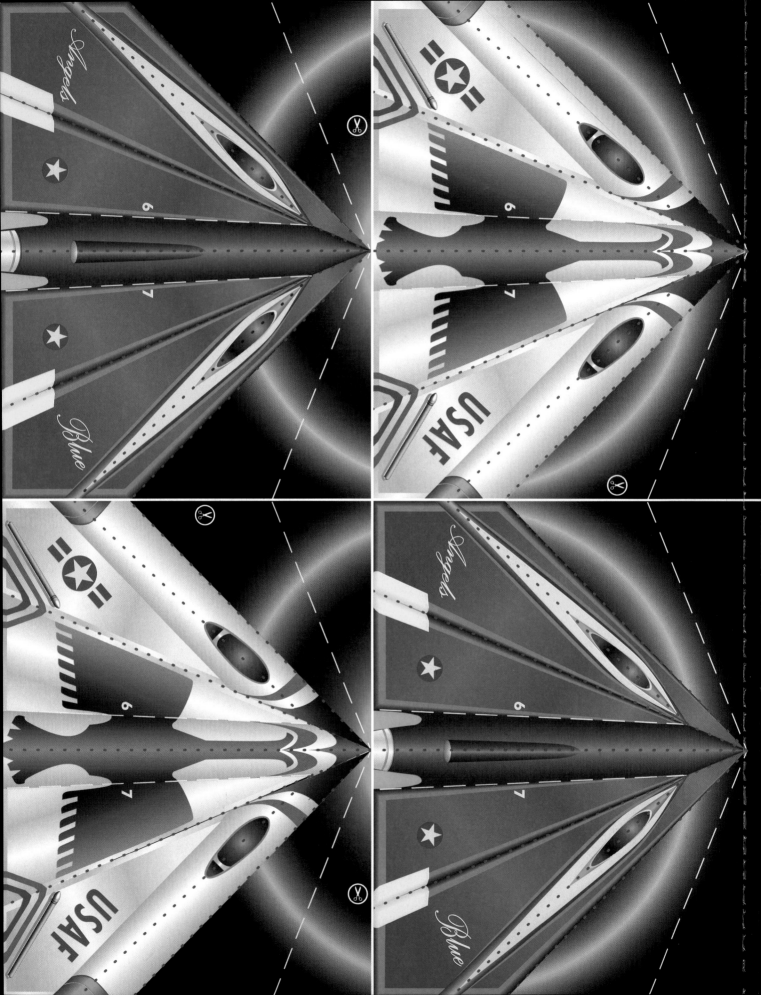

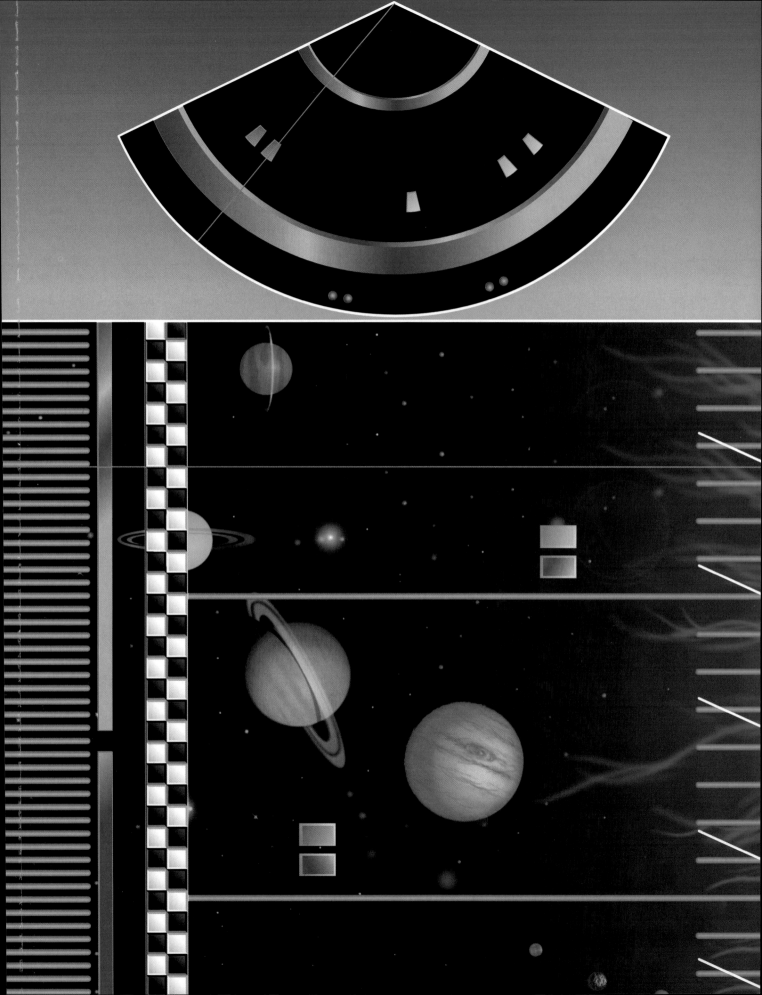

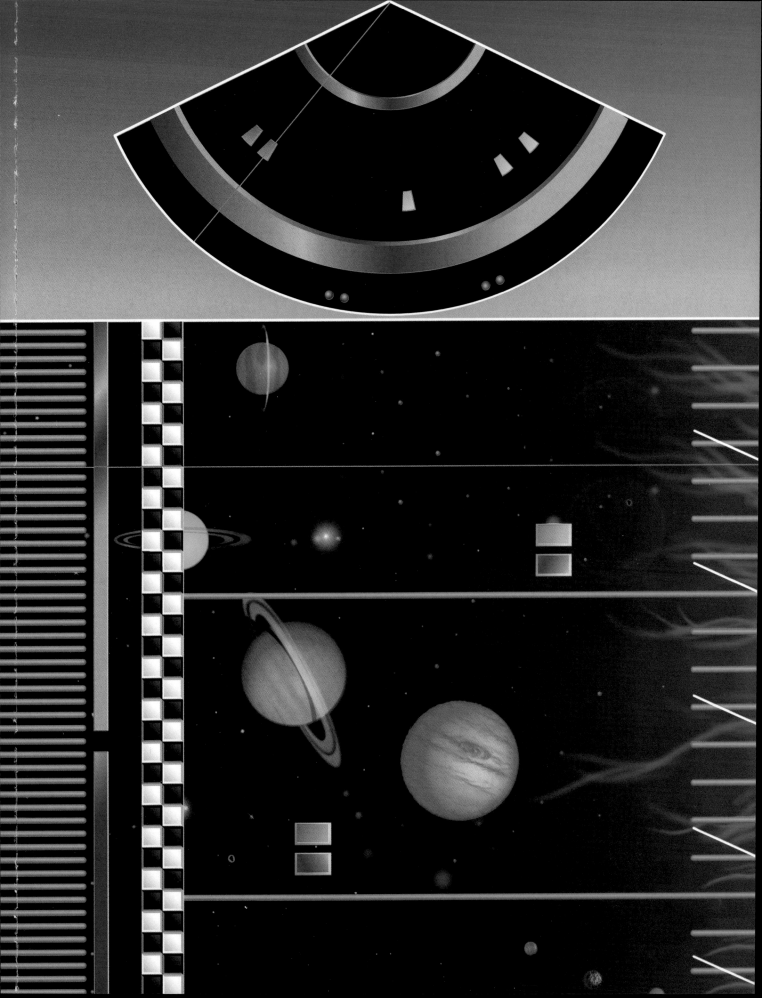

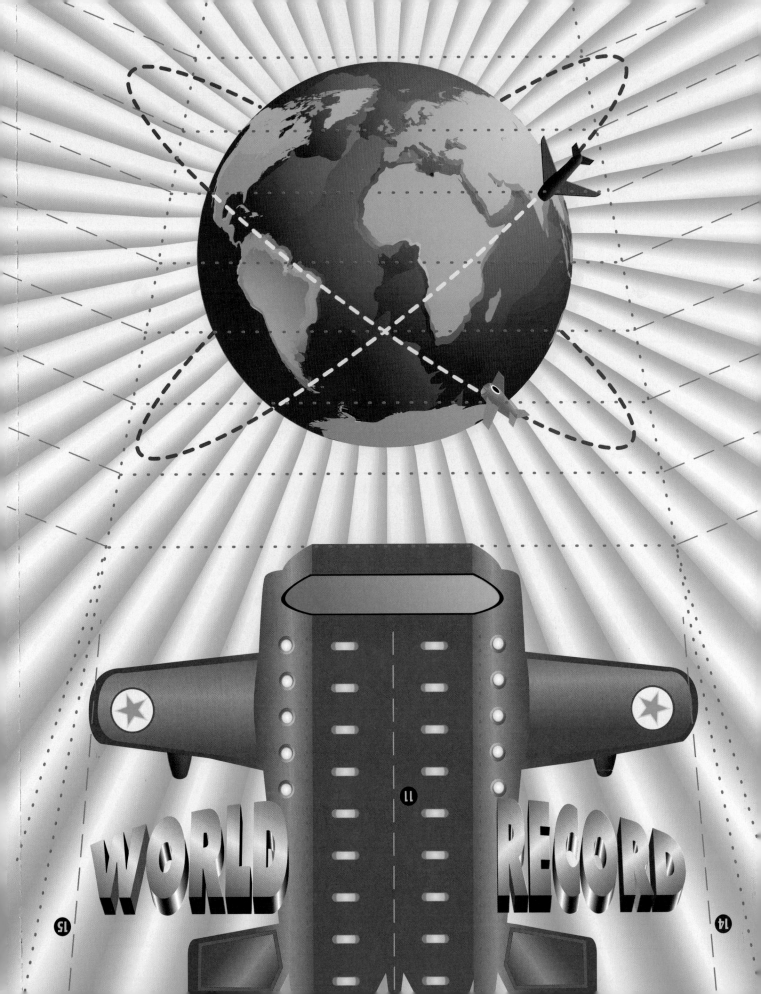

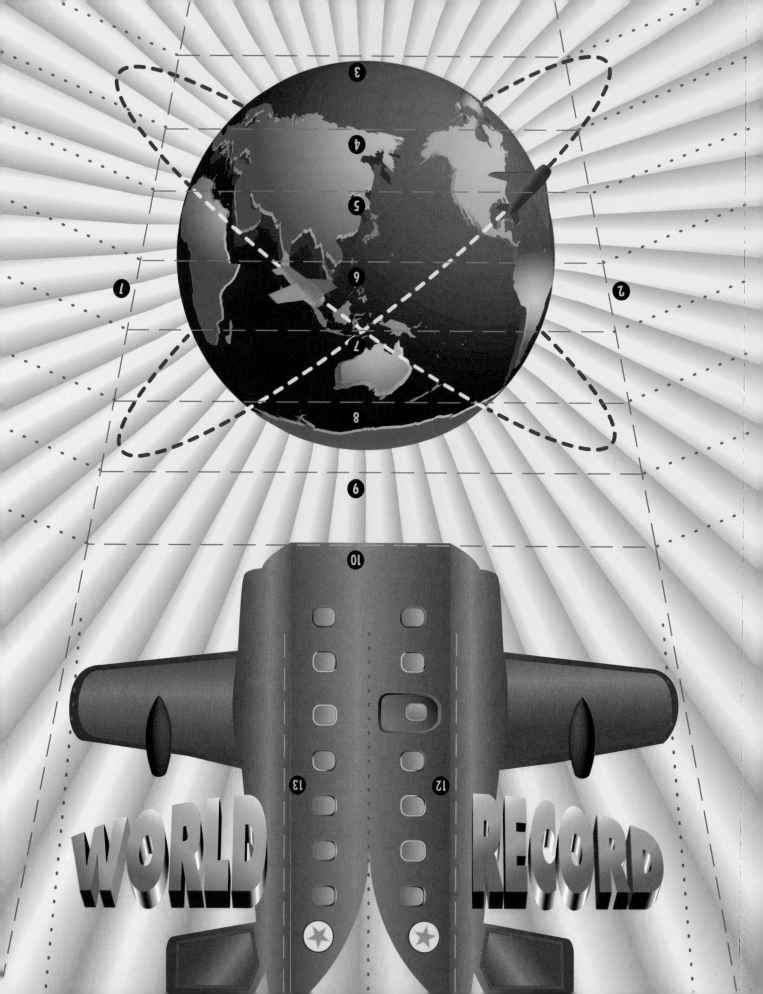

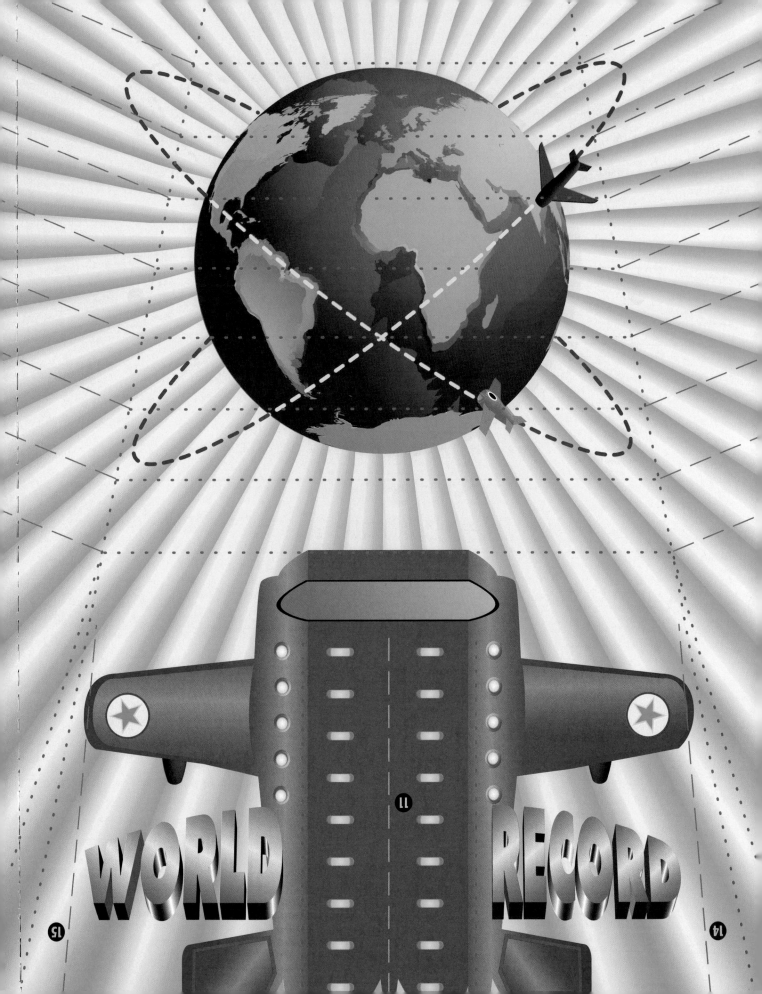

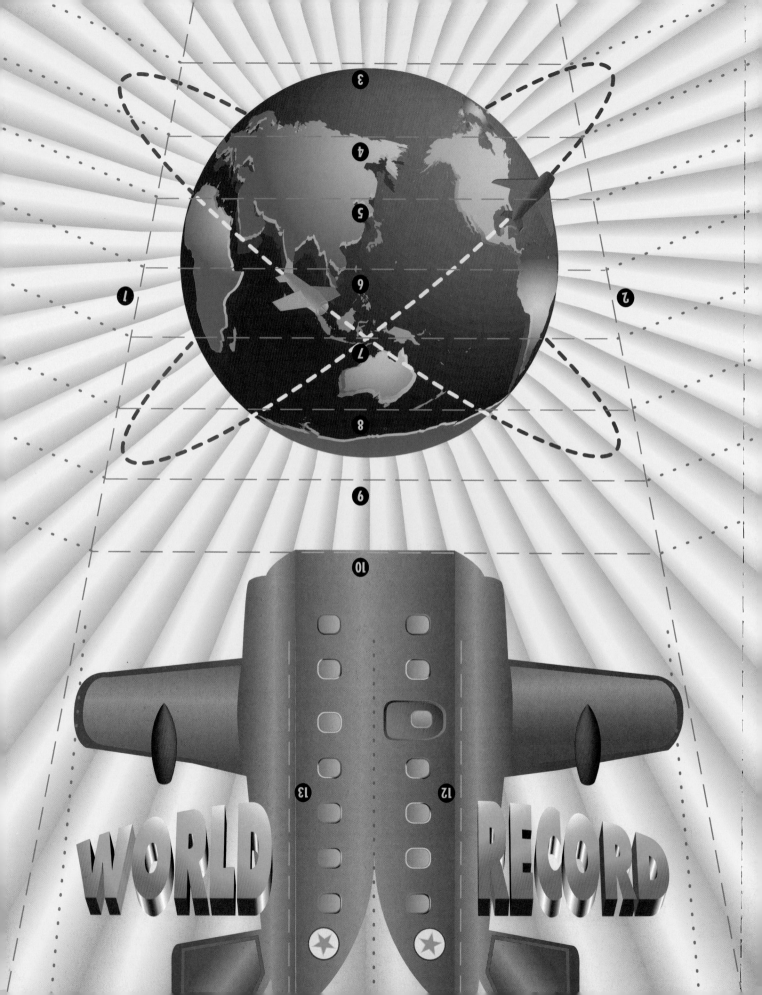

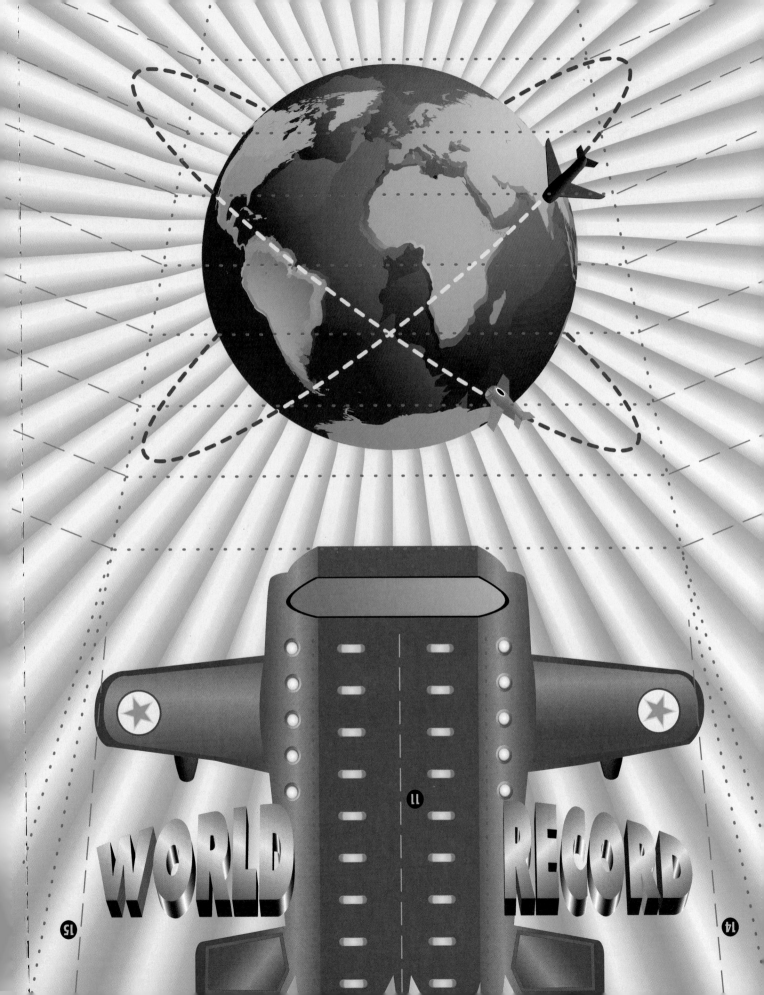

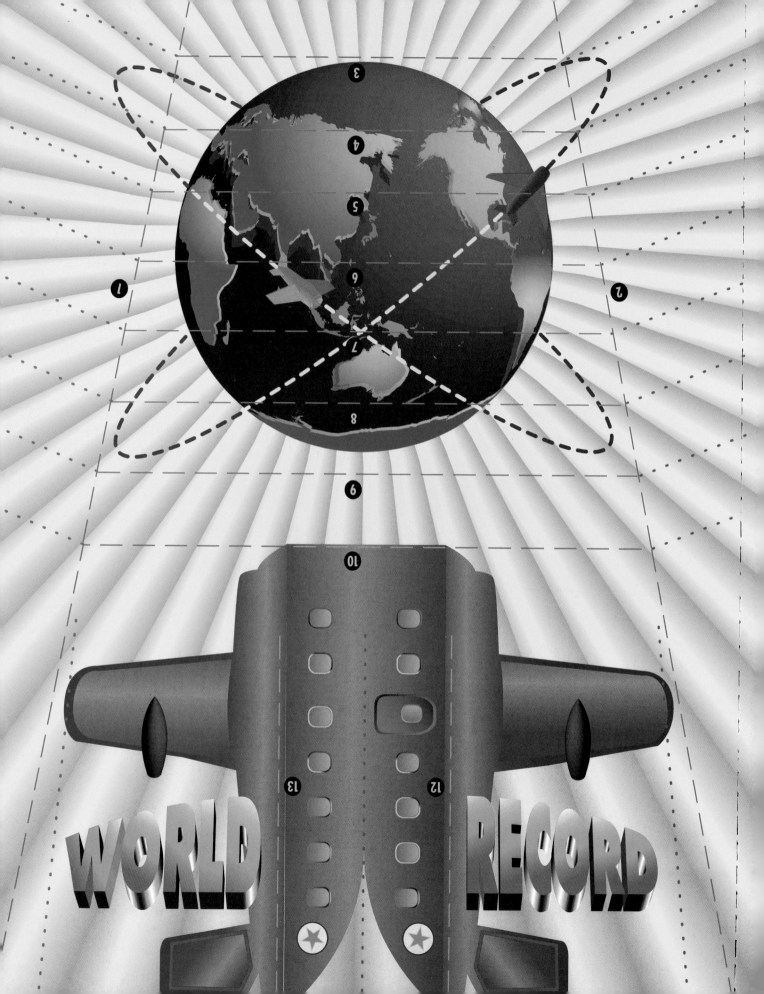

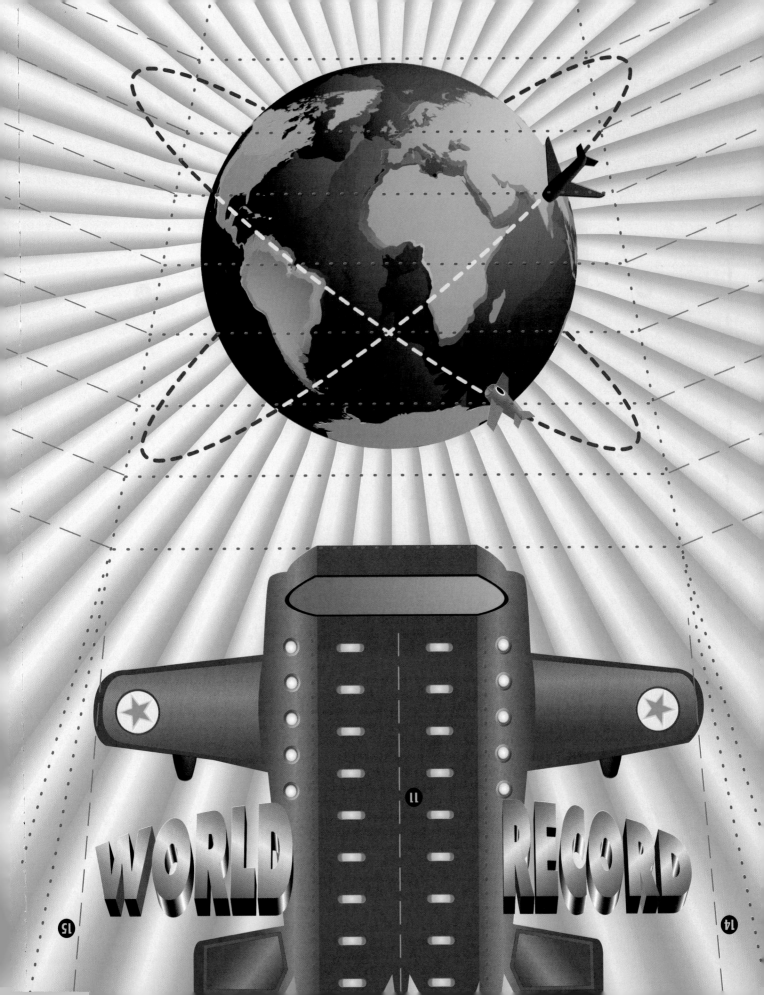

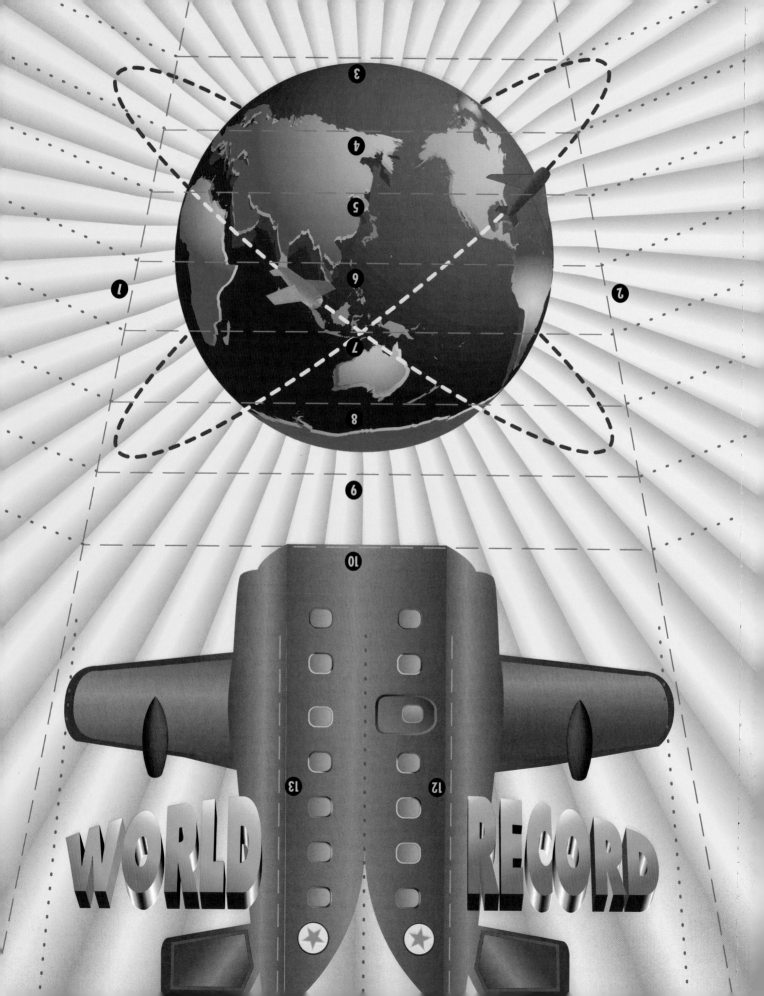

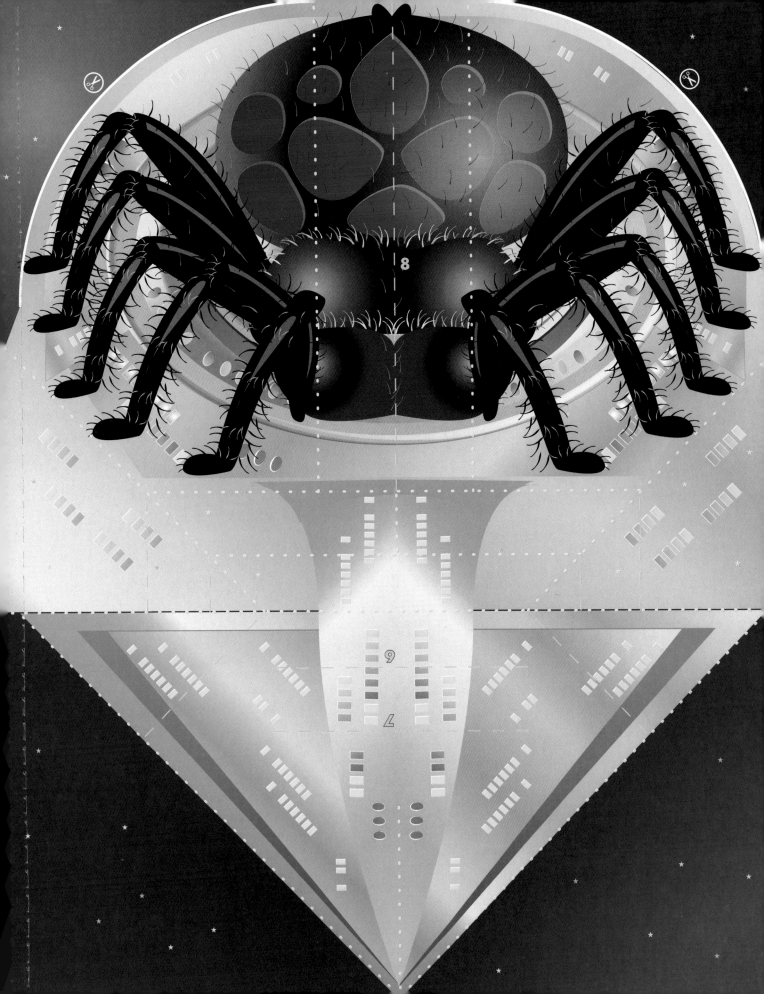

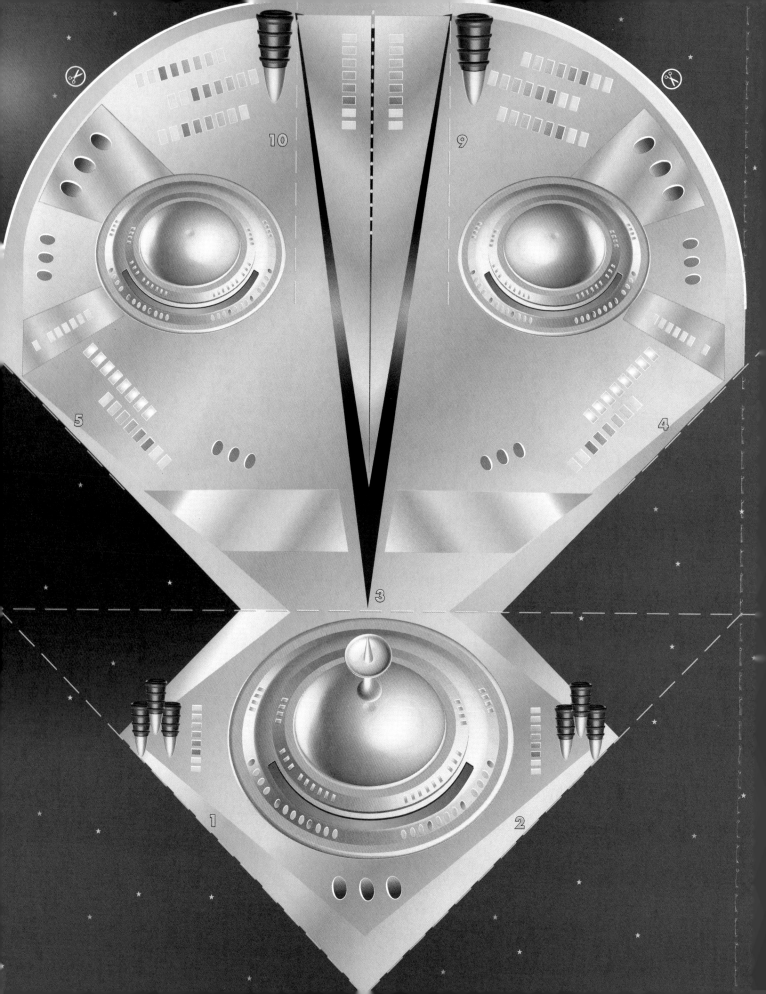

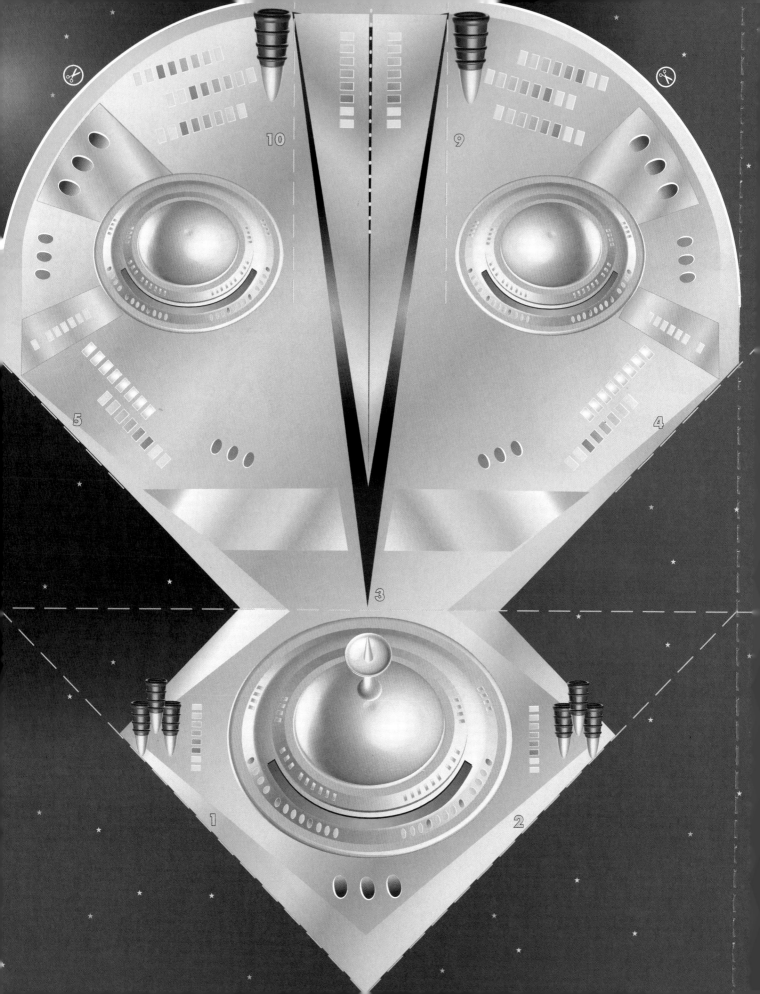

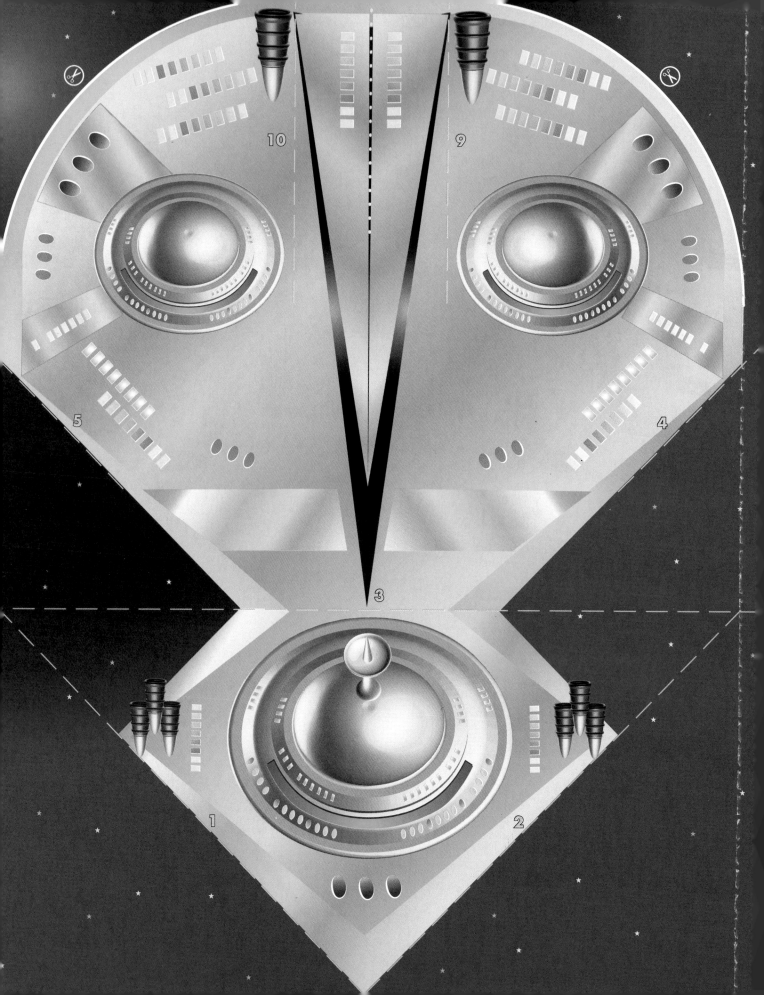

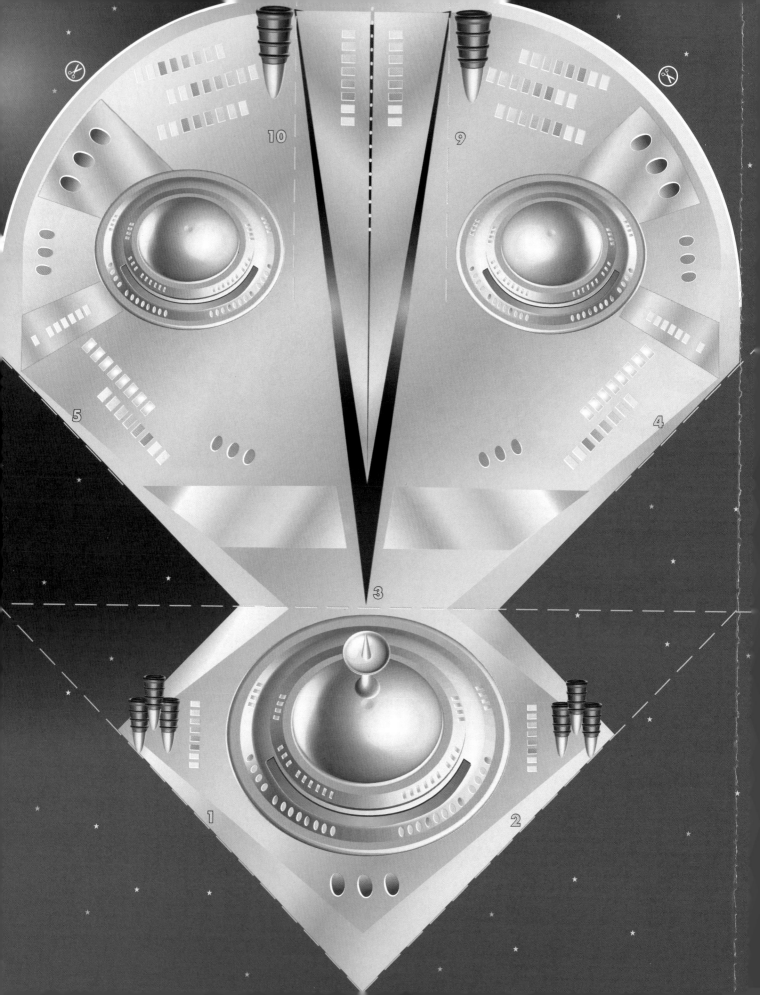

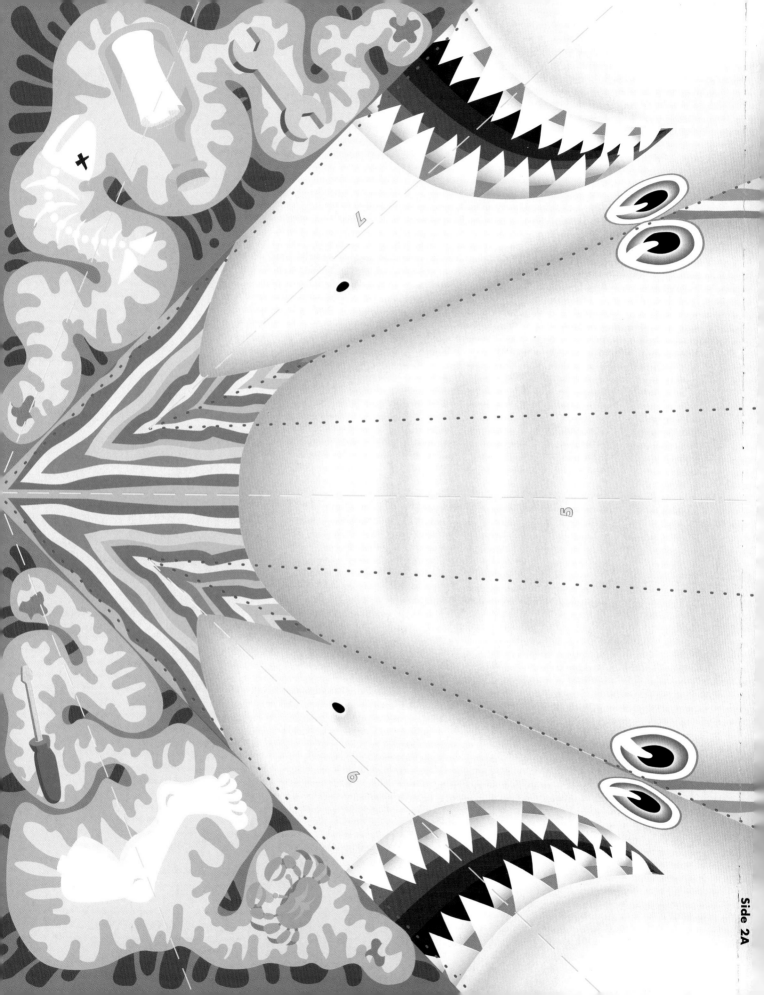

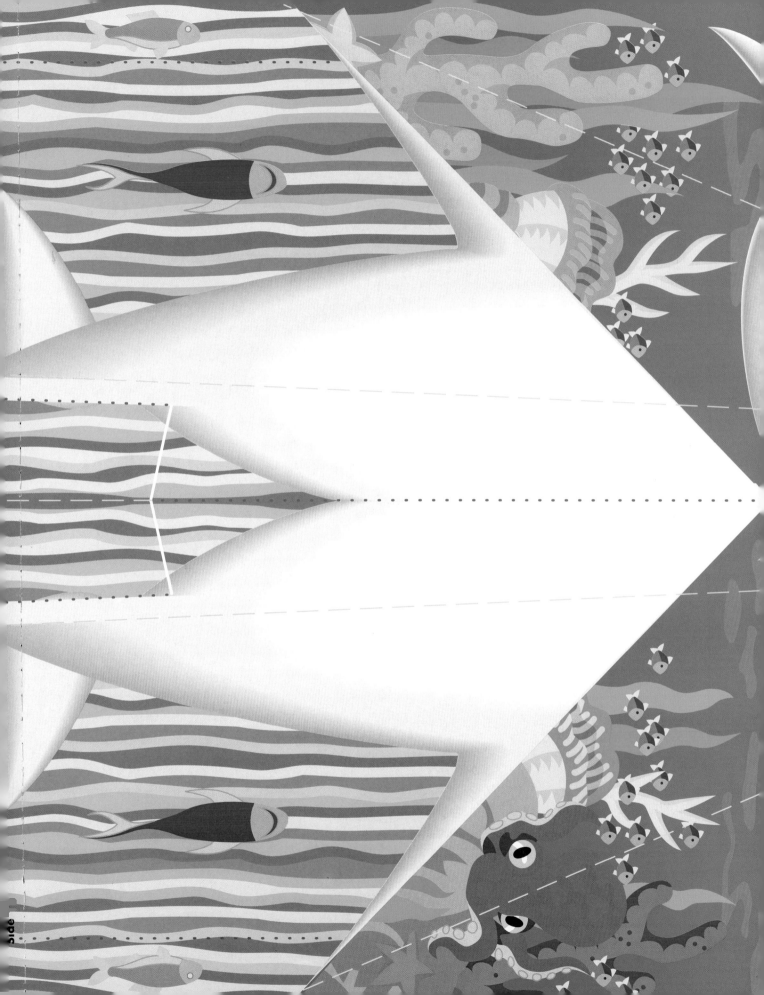

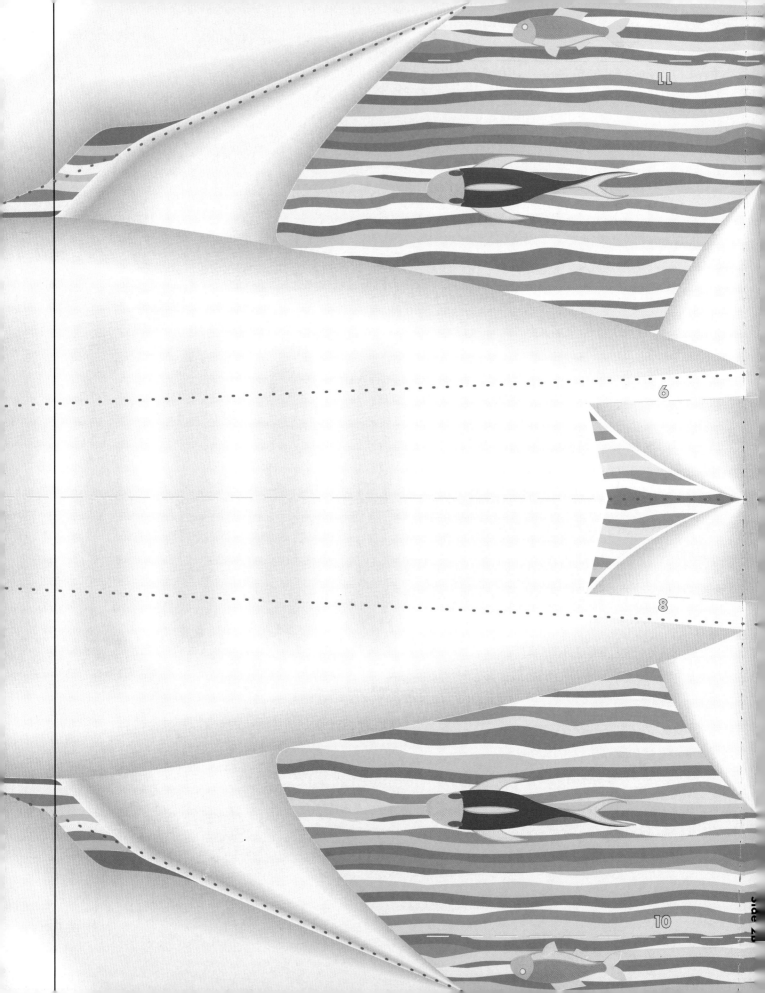

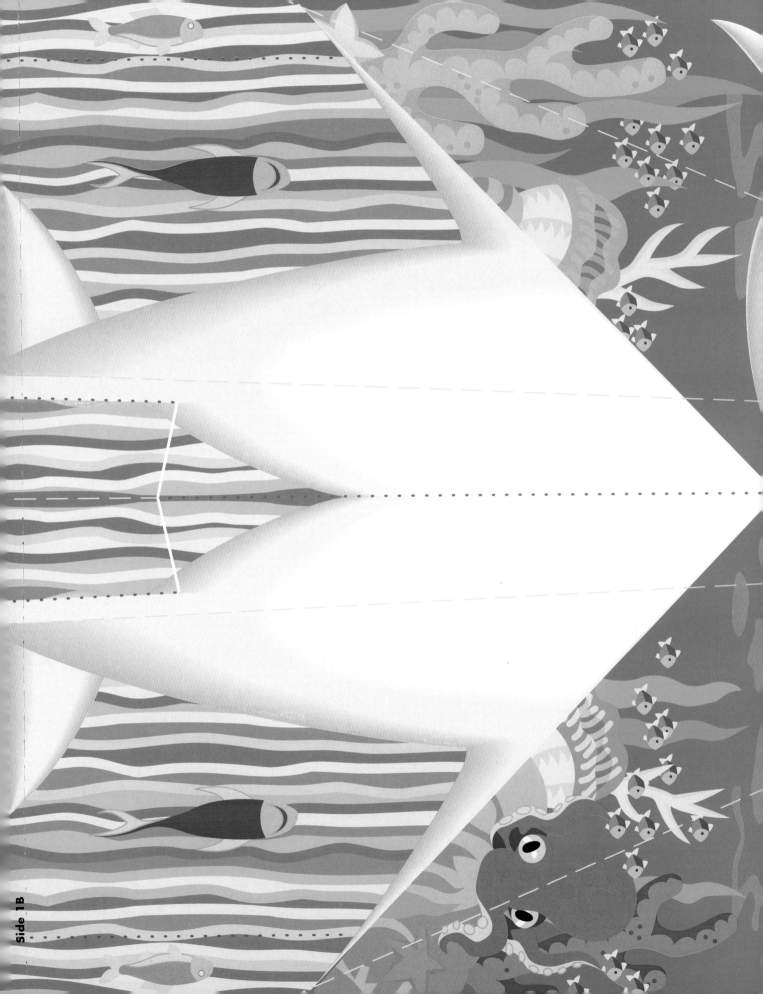

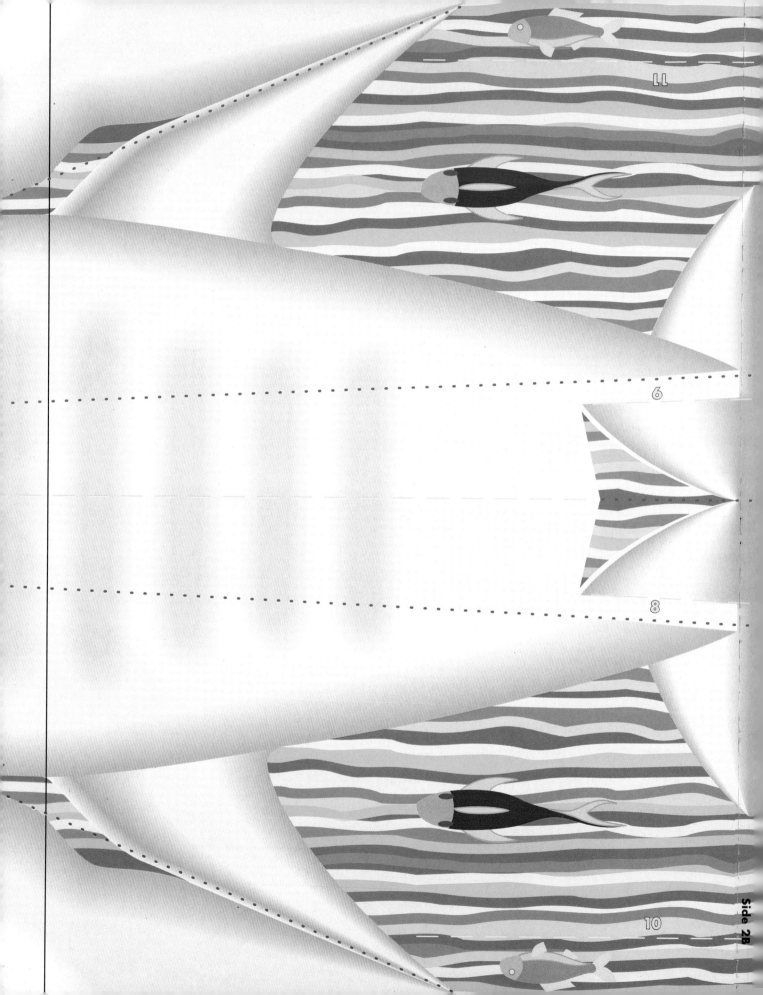

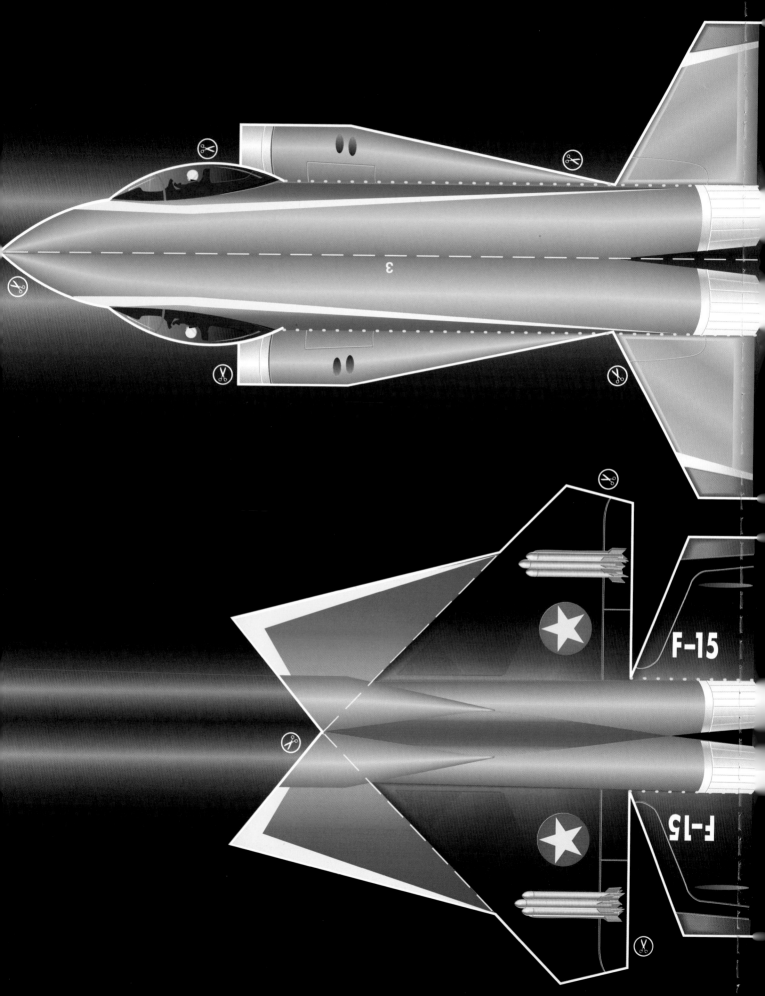

F-15

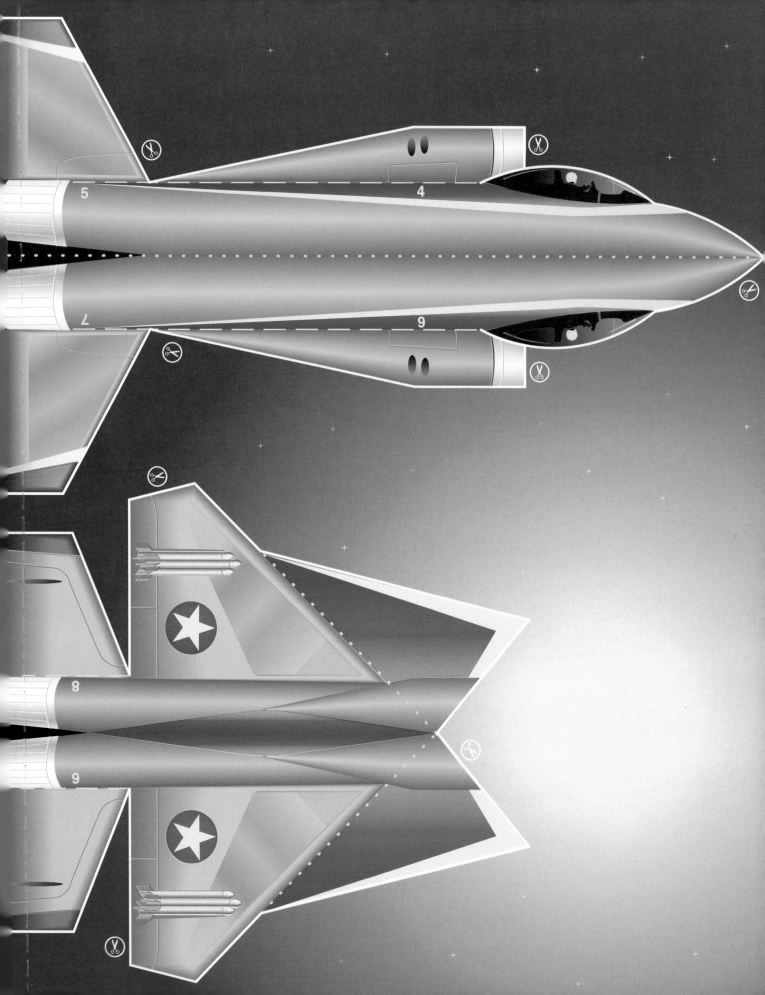

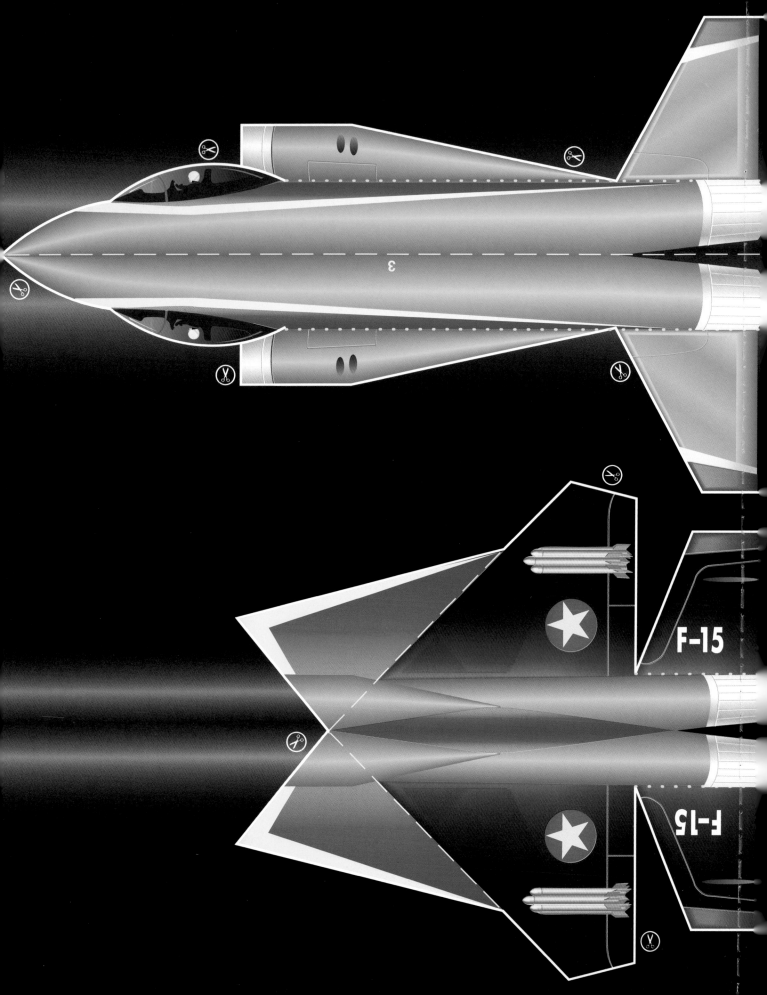

F-15

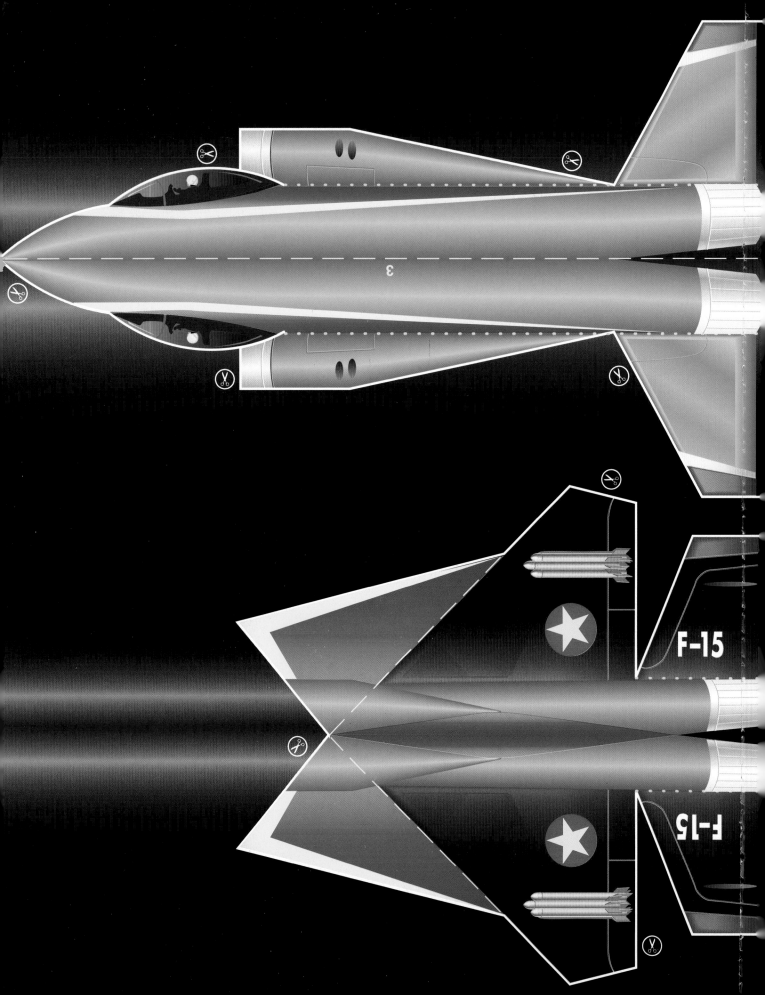